C000137128

THE

COMPLETE OPOS COOKBOOK

Praise for the OPOS cooking technique on Amazon.in

'OPOS fundamentally changed the way I cook.' – *Sneha*

'OPOS has reduced the standing, sautéing and dish washing time; kitchen work is now a breeze. No more scrubbing pots and pans. It's been a blessing for me as a working mother.' – *Rashmi*

'OPOS made me much more organized, gave me extra time for better sleep and helps me to create a huge menu every morning to cater to a wide variety of taste buds!' - *Suchitra Seethapathy*

'The OPOS technique is the most efficient and super-fast way of cooking.' – *Anil G. Walambe*

'OPOS is simple, clean, healthy, efficient and sustainable! And it doesn't involve any expensive equipment. With minimal stuff you are good to go.' – *Mayura Naik*

'Whether you're married or single, man or woman, in a nuclear family or a joint one, OPOS is for each one of you.' – *Neha*

'OPOS is a life-saver.' – *Deepika Vasu*

THE
COMPLETE
OPOS
COOKBOOK

ONE-POT MEAL PLANS
READY IN 10 MINUTES

B. RAMAKRISHNAN

HarperCollins *Publishers* India

First published in India by
HarperCollins *Publishers* in 2021
A-75, Sector 57, Noida, Uttar Pradesh 201301, India
www.harpercollins.co.in

2 4 6 8 10 9 7 5 3

Copyright © B. Ramakrishnan 2021

P-ISBN: 978-93-5357-987-6
E-ISBN: 978-93-5302-995-1

The views and opinions expressed in this book are the author's own and the facts are
as reported by him, and the publishers are not in any way liable for the same.

This book has been published after all reasonable efforts were taken to make the
material error-free. However, the author will not be liable whatsoever for errors and
omissions, whether such errors and omissions result from negligence, accident or
from any other cause or claims for loss or damages of any kind, including without
limitation, indirect or consequential loss or damage arising out of the use, inability
to use, or about the reliability, accuracy or sufficiency of the information contained
in this book. No part of this book shall be used or reproduced in any manner
whatsoever without written permission from the author, except in the case of brief
quotations in articles and book reviews.

All rights reserved. No part of this publication can also be stored in a retrieval system,
or transmitted, in any form or by any means, electronic, mechanical, photocopying,
recording or otherwise, without the prior permission of the publishers.

B. Ramakrishnan asserts the moral right
to be identified as the author of this work.

Typeset in 11/14 Adobe Garamond at
Manipal Technologies Limited, Manipal

Printed and bound at
Thomson Press (India) Ltd

This book is produced from independently certified FSC™paper
to ensure responsible forest management.

श्री भगवानुवाच |
पश्य मे पार्थ रूपाणि शतशोऽथ सहस्रश: |
नानाविधानि दिव्यानि नानावर्णाकृतीनि च ||

śhrī-bhagavān uvācha
paśhya me pārtha rūpāṇi śhataśho 'tha sahasraśhaḥ
nānā-vidhāni divyāni nānā-varṇākṛitīni cha

Behold My Unlimited Divine Forms of Various Hues and Shapes!

Bhagavad Gita, Chapter 11, Verse 5
Vishvarupa Darshana Yoga – The Yoga of the Universal Form

* * *

To the baby OPOStars, our own OPOS army, which will casually
blow away all opposition and take OPOS to every kitchen on earth.

Contents

SECTION III: BEGINNER'S LUCK

SECTION IV: MONDAY TO SUNDAY

SECTION V: WHAT'S IN YOUR FRIDGE

SECTION VI: ONE-SHOT THALIS

SECTION I
INTRODUCTION

What is One Pot One Shot (OPOS) Cooking?

One Pot One Shot or OPOS is a set of scientific cooking techniques designed to unchain you from the kitchen, cut drudgery and empower you to cook confidently. All OPOS recipes use one pot and all cooking is done at one shot. No steps. No supervision. From pastas to Paneer Makhani, Malai Kofta to Mysore Pak, OPOS recipes are easier and faster than cooking instant noodles!

It took us 15 years, 780 blog posts, 26,097 volunteers, 52 children, tonnes of provisions, 1,208 files, 10,411 Facebook posts, 5,601 photos, 320 videos, millions of arguments, 1 dictator, 15 comedians, 1 world record, 4 restaurants, 16 chefs, 14 events and 22 corporate demos before the first OPOS book was published in 2018. We made more progress in the last one year, than we did in the past 15. OPOS became a firm part of thousands of kitchens across the world. It is being shaped and refined by this vast community. You now hold the key to this magical world!

Traditional recipes were not designed for today's lifestyle. Many of us lack the time, skill and support to make traditional recipes work. OPOS replaces manual skill with the right equipment and technique. OPOS standardizes cooking conditions to make all recipes work the same way for anyone, anywhere, anytime. Use standardized equipment and follow recipes to create magic!

How OPOS Works

OPOS is about standardization. Deskilling comes at a price. For OPOS recipes to work, you need to use standard equipment and standardized recipes.

Equipment to get started

OPOS works best with the Pressure Baker, a gas/induction stove, available at www.oposkit.com, where you will also get measuring cups and spoons, and a weighing scale.

The Pressure Baker is a supercharged version of a pressure cooker, designed to cook without water and over high heat. It cooks 500 g of almost all vegetables in under 5 minutes. It also supports Cold Pressure Frying (p. 44).

A couple of 2L cookers is all you need for a small family. The 2L can cook breakfast/lunch/dinner (pongal/upma/rice/biryani/pasta/noodles/porridge) for two; dry or gravy curries and soups for four; starters (fondue/stuffed vegetables/kadhai paneer/pindi chana/pepper chicken) for five; pickles/jam/desserts for ten; and hard-boiled eggs for 15. The best part is, it can cook all the above in 5 to 10 minutes!

If you need to cook more, go for a 3L Pressure Baker, which is bigger. The 4.5L OPOS Pressure Baker is ideal for rice/meat-based recipes. Then CookBot, an automated version of the Pressure Baker, is also available on our website.

OPOS cookware is not mandatory for all OPOS recipes. You can use your normal 2L/3L pressure cooker for basic recipes. Choose models that are broad and shallow; avoid tall and narrow designs and a size larger than 3L as they invariably overcook vegetables.

However, please note that normal pressure cookers are not designed to be used on high heat or without water. They still work with basic OPOS recipes if you are careful, but it is risky using them for advanced lessons. Skip recipes like Ghee, Sugar Syrup-based recipes and Cold Pressure Frying if you are using normal cookware, as it is not designed to handle them.

The Pressure Baker is a supercharged version of a pressure cooker; the CookBot is its automated version.

Measuring ingredients accurately is critical for success when you OPOS it. Use standard measuring cups, spoons (1 cup = 240ml, 1tsp = 5ml, 1tbsp = 15ml) and a kitchen scale. Use measuring cups for liquids and a weighing scale for solids, especially in tricky recipes like sugar syrup.

Shopping list

This kitchen pantry list below includes many of the items you will need to prepare the OPOS recipes featured in this book.

Starch Rice, poha, vermicelli, pasta, noodles, puffed rice, rava, wheat flour, rice flour, millet, oats, sago.

Protein Tuvar (arhar) dal, moong dal, chana dal, chickpeas, kidney beans, green peas, gram flour, roasted gram, soya chunks, whole moong, sprouts, paneer, mushroom, chicken, mutton, other meats, fish, seafood and eggs.

Micronutrients Onion, tomato, fresh vegetables, spinach.

Fats Ghee, virgin oils (sesame, coconut, peanut), mustard oil, refined vegetable oils.

Dairy Butter, cream, milk, yogurt, condensed milk.

Spice Box Garam masala, chilli, coriander, cumin, turmeric, asafoetida (hing), sambar, pepper powders, mustard, fenugreek, fennel seeds, cardamom, cinnamon, bay leaf, cloves, ginger, garlic, dry fenugreek leaves, urad dal, dry red chilli.

Essentials Salt, sugar, pickles, papad, tamarind, coconut, chilli, coconut milk, coconut milk powder, cashews, peanuts.

Optional Cheese, almonds, raisins, sesame, saffron, cinnamon, Italian seasoning.

Why OPOS?

The OPOS promise

OPOS is Green. One pot to wash.

OPOS is Clean. Hygienic. Less mess.

OPOS is Fast. Fresh food in minutes.

OPOS is Liberating. No supervision.

OPOS is Healthy. Maximizes nutrition.

OPOS is Flexible. Cook your way.

OPOS is Economical. Saves fuel and water.

OPOS is Tasty. Intense flavours.

OPOS is Transparent. Works for all.

OPOS is Consistent. Works every time.

OPOS is Universal. Cooks all cuisines!

Tried and tested

Every single OPOS recipe is debated, tested, fine-tuned and validated hundreds of times by members of OPOS School and OPOS Support Group Facebook communities. The work of this passionate group of doctors, nutritionists, dieticians, bloggers, authors, chefs, food stylists, artists, homemakers, actors, scientists, caterers and many others continues to shape OPOS.

OPOS is not a fancy word for pressure cooking

Very few OPOS recipes follow the 'dump all into a cooker' technique. Most OPOS recipes are built on Pressure Baking, a brand-new cooking technique developed for OPOS where food is cooked in its own juices, over high heat, for a very short time. Similar to stir-frying, it is much faster than normal pressure cooking. Pressure Baking combined with other OPOS techniques is responsible for the intense colour, flavour, taste and textures of OPOS dishes.

Key OPOS techniques you need to know

Bottled Tadka

Frying spices for tadka can be problematic, especially if you don't live in India. Bottled Tadka is the best solution for this.

Before getting into OPOS tadka, let us understand how a tadka works.

All herbs and spices derive their flavour from aromatic compounds. When added, these compounds impart their flavour to food. Some of these compounds dissolve in water, others in oil. Those that dissolve in water can be added directly. Those that dissolve in oil need to be steeped in oil till their flavours are extracted.

There are two ways to infuse an oil with flavour – hot infusion and cold infusion. Indian cuisine infuses sesame/ coconut / peanut/ mustard oil / ghee with mustard seeds, cumin, curry leaves, chillies, garlic, ginger, cardamom, cloves, star anise, bay leaves, fennel, fenugreek etc., to create hot oil infusions or the tadka.

The Bottled Tadka is very simple. You can do it in an open pan or OPOS it. Just make a large quantity of it and bottle it. Mix with food before/after cooking.

For Bottled Tadka recipes, see p. 26.

Controlled Caramelization

Onions/ tomatoes form the base for a huge range of recipes, so we desperately needed a hack to eliminate the sauteeing step which tied generations of cooks to the stove for hours. We achieved it with the Controlled Caramelization technique.

The key to onion caramelization is pyrolysis, a decomposition of organic compounds at high heats. The logic is simple – we had to heat onions so that the complex sugars in them break down into simpler sugars. This browns them, makes them sweeter and much more flavourful. This heating needs to stop just short of burning and needs to be unsupervised.

Controlled caramelization made it possible for us to create the base for many recipes, in a single step, in under 5 minutes of unsupervised cooking.

For our Controlled Caramelization recipe, see p. 23.

Inner pot or Pot-in-Pot (PIP)

This technique of using inner vessels gives us great control in cooking different things together. It's used for various reasons:

- To isolate cooking inhibitors such as tamarind, jaggery and sugar (e.g., Sambar).
- To prevent curdling when cooking dairy with ingredients that may cause it to curdle (e.g., Kuruma with milk).
- To promote caramelization while cooking caramelized curries with starch (e.g., Pasta with sauce).
- To create two separate heating zones. By nesting many pots, we can cook almost everything together, irrespective of their cooking time.
- To isolate non-edible stuff from edible stuff (e.g., Arbi Masala).
- To create multiple dishes (e.g., One-shot Thalis, see p. 24).
- In recipes where part of the ingredients need to be blended, an inner vessel is easier to remove.
- For double boiling.
- To hold watery spice pastes.
- In recipes with just an oil buffer, a small inner vessel with tadka ingredients and oil can simulate open pot frying perfectly.

Layering

OPOS is science – but layering elevates it to an artform. We arrange ingredients in a very precise manner based on how they cook. We need to completely visualize the cooking process in our heads before we can start layering. In traditional cooking, layering is not given much importance as you can constantly supervise cooking and can make changes at any point.

OPOStars (the OPOS technique innovators) spend an enormous amount of time in learning to rewrite traditional recipes with the right layering format. Layering was initially introduced when many members faced burning while cooking no water recipes. All recipes were then re-standardized to use a thin layer of buffer as the bottom layer. The next layer suggested was a watery ingredient like onion/ tomato/other watery vegetables/ meats. Easy to burn ingredients like starches, dals, coconut, dry spice powders, etc., are never used as the bottom layer.

For tips on Layering, see p. 21.

For a quick guide to all our techniques, see p. 243.

Minimal Prep Work

After cooking time was brought to under 5 minutes for many recipes, we had to address food preparation. Chopping took much longer than cooking.

This problem can be addressed in two ways. Either generate a series of recipes using ingredients which require no cutting or use a grater/slicer/blender to mechanize cutting.

- Ingredients that require no cutting: Choose bases that require no cutting and pair them with additives and flavouring that do not require a knife.
- A huge variety of veggies/meats are available as ready to use. These can be used whole/snapped/torn with hand/crushed/grated/sliced.
- Ingredients that can be used whole: Baby potatoes, mushrooms, baby carrots, cherry tomatoes, baby corn, Brussels sprouts,

asparagus, soya chunks, soaked legumes, sprouts, fresh legumes, ladyfinger, eggs, etc.

- Vegetables that can be snapped and used: French beans, broad beans, long beans, cluster beans, cauliflower, broccoli, baby radish, etc.
- Ingredients that can be torn, crushed or crumbled and used: Spinach varieties, capsicum, paneer, tofu, etc.
- Vegetables that can be crushed and used: Mushroom, tomato, garlic.
- Vegetables that can be grated and used: Carrot, radish, tomato, potato, squash, beets, turnip, etc.
- Vegetables that can be sliced and used: Ivy gourd, carrot, radish, cabbage, brinjal, bitter gourd, capsicum, snake gourd, onion.
- Others that come pre-cut: Chopped meats/cleaned seafood.

Pressure Bake these and pair with starches to make breakfast, lunch or dinner.

Flavouring

Rely mostly on dry powders/crushed spices/herbs.

Additives

- Avoid additives that require chopping.
- Use curry bases, pickles, nut pastes, dairy, coconut paste, cooked lentils, tamarind paste, etc., that can be paired with most ingredients to create a variety of recipes.

Avoid hard-to-prep vegetables

- Skip vegetables like banana flower or banana stem unless you have time on hand.
- Choose easy vegetables: Cabbage, gourds, mushroom, potato, carrot, baby vegetables, radish, drumstick, ladyfinger.
- Beans: Chop off ends and use whole.

- Yam, squash, beetroot: Use a peeler and peel skin.
- Greens: Soak in lots of water. Shake well to remove sand. Chop off roots and chop coarsely.
- Onion: Slice with skin. Wash to remove skin.
- Garlic, ginger: Blend with skin.

Cut

The cut does not matter in OPOS as long as it is not too thick. The way vegetables are cut have little effect on their taste. Ignore rules on sambar-cut, aviyal-cut, etc. Cut the same way for everything. Try crushing vegetables. You get interesting textures!

Avoid peeling

Almost all vegetable peels barring a few, especially tubers, are edible and nutritious. Never peel vegetables except in cases of arbi (taro root), yam, etc., where the peels are not edible.

Chop right

Have a good peeler and grater. Get a good, heavy knife. The heavier the knife, the lesser the strain on your wrist. Learn chopping. With the right technique, it is effortless.

Abbreviations and acronyms

tsp	Teaspoon
tbsp	Tablespoon
C	Cup (Standard Why OPOS? = 240ml)
g	Gram
mins	Minutes

wh	Whistles
PIP	Pot in Pot: An OPOS technique where ingredients are placed in a small vessel and kept inside the Pressure Baker.

Avoid trouble!

Start with Lesson 1.

Use standard equipment and follow the recipe to the letter.

Go by whistles or timing, whichever comes first.

Never force open a pressurized pot.

If steam leaks or if you smell burning, switch off, check, add water and continue.

Watch videos (search for OPOS videos on Google/YouTube).

Join the OPOS Support Group on Facebook and follow discussions.

Download the OPOS Chef app for more recipes.

Visit OPOSChef on YouTube

Visit OPOS FB Support Group

OPOS FAQs

Most questions we get translate to: 'Can you teach me OPOS with the equipment I have, the way I like, using methods I am comfortable with?'

We can't! OPOS recipes need to work exactly the same way for anyone, anywhere, anytime. Else, they lose the OPOS tag.

What is the serving size of your recipes?

Almost all recipes serve 2. Most recipes can be scaled up proportionately to serve 4 but this will result in marginal overcooking. For scaling up, the general rule of thumb is to double all and go by whistles if you don't mind overcooking. Else use another pot or cook again.

How to scale-up?

Once you understand the basic techniques, you can easily figure out the way to use bigger cookers or scale-up. Till then, please stick to the recipes. Cook multiple times instead of scaling-up. If you do scale-up, scale up everything, including the cooker size and go by the number of whistles.

- It is easier than you think. Remember to scale-up everything proportionately. You need to make sure the quantity you cook matches the pot size.
- Ensure your pot is at least 1/4 full and not over 3/4 full.
- In all scaled-up recipes, the timing will vary but the number of whistles remains the same.

- Use more water than necessary for the first try. All recipes using water can be scaled-up safely.
- No-water recipes are tricky and need monitoring the first time. Watch out for a burnt smell.
- Use the same heat setting as you used when standardizing your 2L cooker. Increase heat once you get comfortable.

I was always doing OPOS, without knowing the name!

You have been pressure cooking. Welcome to Pressure Baking – a whole new technique, the complete opposite of pressure cooking. Multi-step cooking or dumping all in a cooker is not OPOS. Be ready to unlearn all you know and start afresh.

These fancy shortcut techniques can't match the taste of traditional recipes!

OPOS is not about shortcuts/quick cooking. It is a way to bring the best out of food. We are fortunate that it also works so quickly! Techniques like Pressure Baking and layering unlocked a burst of colour, flavour and texture never seen before! Every single OPOS technique added a bit of magic. Now OPOS not just matches traditional recipes, it far outclasses them in most cases. Many of us suddenly find non-OPOS food tasteless!

Why does one OPOS dish have multiple recipes?

All OPOS recipes work, but the newer ones work better. This is because each recipe is being continually polished. The layering, quantities and many other details keep getting fine-tuned based on feedback from our community.

Where am I going wrong?

These are the top reasons why OPOS recipes fail:

- Use of non-standard equipment.
- Not using measuring cups, spoons/weighing scales.

- Cutting food into big chunks.
- Not tracking time/whistles.
- Adding/omitting ingredients, or changing quantities.
- Trying to personalize a recipe at the first attempt.
- Not understanding the techniques behind the recipes.

In other words, you failed because you did not follow the recipe to the T. All this can be avoided with a bit of discipline. The only reason why some recipes might still fail is because the ingredients we use are different. There is no solution for this but to understand the technique and tweak the recipe.

One step at a time!

OPOSing requires discipline. Start with Lesson 1 and take one step at a time.

1. Cook to learn
2. Cook to eat
3. Cook to feed
4. Cook to impress

There are no shortcuts for these stages!

SECTION II
CORE LESSONS AND STAPLES

Pressure Baking Basics

All recipes in this book have been prepared using standardized equipment. Please complete Lesson 1 to ascertain the 'high'* setting for your equipment, Lesson 2 to understand Pressure Baking – the core technique upon which all other OPOS techniques are built, followed by the other lessons in this section before proceeding further.**

LESSON 1: STANDARDIZATION

To ensure your equipment is suitable for OPOS, standardization puts us all on the same page

In a 2L OPOS Pressure Baker, add 1/4 cup water. Close, fix weight and switch on the stove. Cook on 'high' to 1 whistle between 1 and 2 minutes. Switch off.

Tips

- Hear 1 whistle in less than 1 minute? Reduce heat.
- Hear 1 whistle after 2 minutes? Increase heat.
- On gas, ensure the flame covers the base of your Pressure Baker without coming up the sides.
- Cooker handle heating up? Change burner/use induction.

---

* Whenever the recipe mentions 'high', it refers to this setting. This will vary depending on the heat source. On induction cooker, 'high' is around 1200W.

** A 2L OPOS Pressure Baker has been used unless otherwise mentioned.

- Electric/ceramic stovetops are sluggish and need 5 to 15 minutes of preheating before you place the Pressure Baker over it.

How Pressure Baking Works

LESSON 2: VEGETABLES

Learning the 'High-heat, Low-time, No-water' OPOS Mantra

Beans

In a 2L Pressure Baker, layer as below:
Layer 1: 1/4 cup water, 1tsp oil
Layer 2: 2 cups chopped beans
Layer 3: 1/2tsp salt, 1 chopped green chilli

Close, fix weight and switch on the stove. Cook on high for 2 whistles or 4 minutes, whichever comes first. Switch off stove. Release pressure by gently lifting the weight. Open. Mix everything. Marvel at the colour. The 1/4 cup water you add is for beginners, as an insurance against burning. Most fresh vegetables/meats can be Pressure Baked in their own juices, with very little or no water.

Tips

- Substitute beans with your favourite vegetables.
- Tough vegetables like potato need to be cut smaller.
- Edible greens shrink dramatically.
- Ladyfinger needs to be wiped dry, cut big and Pressure Baked only with oil to avoid sliminess.
- Excess water? Repeat by reducing water.

- Watery vegetables leak water? Chop them bigger.
- Undercooked? Mix everything and rest. Will cook in retained heat. Or cook for one more whistle.

LESSON 3: MEALS

Pressure Bake and Mix in Starch

Tava Pulav

In a 2L Pressure Baker, layer as below:
Layer 1: 1/4 cup water, 1tsp oil
Layer 2: 2 chopped green chillies, 1 cup each chopped small (beans, carrot)
Layer 3: 1/2tsp each (salt, garam masala powder)

Close, fix weight and switch on the stove. Cook on high for 2 whistles or 4 minutes, whichever comes first. Switch off stove. Release pressure by gently lifting the weight. Open. Mix everything. Mix in 3 cups starch (cooked and cooled rice/chopped roti/cooked pasta/washed and drained poha/puffed rice/chopped bread).

LESSON 4: SOUPS

Pressure Bake and Blend

Carrot Soup

In a 2L Pressure Baker, layer as below:
Layer 1: 2tbsp oil
Layer 2: 2 chopped green chillies
Layer 3: 2 cups finely chopped carrot
Layer 4: 1/2tsp each (salt, garam masala powder, pepper powder)

Close, fix weight and switch on the stove. Cook on high for 2 whistles or 4 minutes, whichever comes first. Switch off stove. Release pressure by gently lifting the weight. Open. Add 2 cups hot water. Blend everything to a smooth liquid.

LESSON 5: MASHES

Pressure Bake Mixed Vegetables and Mash

Pav Bhaji

In a 2L Pressure Baker, layer as below:
Layer 1: 1/4 cup water, 1tbsp butter
Layer 2: 2 chopped green chillies
Layer 3: 1 cup each chopped small (potato, beans, carrot)
Layer 4: 1/4 cup finely chopped beetroot
Layer 5: 1/2tsp each (salt, garam masala powder)

Close, fix weight and switch on the stove. Cook on high for 3 whistles or 5 minutes, whichever comes first. Switch off stove. Release pressure by gently lifting the weight. Open. Mash everything to a coarse paste. Serve with toasted bread/pav.

LESSON 6: GRAVIES

Pressure Bake With a Curry Paste Layer

Egg Kuruma

Prep.: Blend 10 cashewnuts, 3 chopped green chillies, 1/2tsp each (salt, garam masala powder) 1tsp oil, 1/4 cup water to a thick paste.

In a 2L Pressure Baker, layer as below:
Layer 1: 1/4 cup water, 1tbsp ghee
Layer 2: 1 cup each chopped small (potato, beans, carrot)
Layer 3: Pot in Pot (PIP) – Spice paste (see prep.). Fit in two well-washed eggs over the vegetables (optional)

Close, fix weight and switch on the stove. Cook on high for 3 whistles or 5 minutes, whichever comes first. Switch off stove. Release pressure by gently lifting the weight. Open. Remove eggs. Mix spice paste with vegetables. Mix in 1/4 cup milk/coconut milk to dilute. Let eggs cool. Peel and halve. Add to gravy.

LESSON 7: CURRY BASES

Controlled Caramelization

Onion–Tomato Mother Sauce

In a 2L Pressure Baker, layer as below:
Layer 1: 1/4 cup oil
Layer 2: 1 cup chopped onion, 5 each whole (small tomatoes, peeled garlic cloves, green chillies), 2tbsp chopped ginger, 1/2tsp salt

Close, fix weight and switch on the stove. Cook on high for 5 whistles or 4 minutes, whichever comes first. Switch off stove. Release pressure by gently lifting the weight. Open. Add 1tsp Kashmiri chilli powder, 1/2tsp garam masala powder. Mash everything. Bottle.

Tips

- Cook longer if you need more caramelization.
- If using big tomatoes, cut them in half and scoop out the seeds.
- Sliced onions caramelize faster.
- Ensure tomato and garlic touch the base so that they caramelize.
- If onions are too watery, slice, mix in 1/4tsp salt and squeeze them to remove excess water before adding.
- Can drain excess oil on opening.

LESSON 8: MEATS

Mutton Sukka

In a 2L Pressure Baker, layer as below:
Layer 1: 2tbsp oil
Layer 2: 1/2 cup whole, peeled shallots, 250g boneless mutton chopped small
Layer 3: 1/2tsp each (salt, chilli powder, garam masala powder, pepper), 1tsp ginger-garlic paste, a pinch of turmeric powder

Close, fix weight and switch on the stove. Cook on high for 25 whistles or 8 minutes, whichever comes first. Switch off stove. Let pressure settle. Open. Mix everything.

Tips

- Overcooked? Reduce cooking time/dice bigger.
- Undercooked? Increase cooking time, dice smaller, use tender meat.

The separator allows you to cook multiple dishes together.

LESSON 9: ONE-SHOT THALIS

Zoned Pressure Baking

In a 2L Pressure Baker, add 1/4 cup water. Place separators to divide it into three zones.

In zone 1, add 1 cup chopped beans, 1/4tsp salt, 1tsp chopped chilli. In zone 2, add 1 cup potato chopped small, 1 scooped tomato filled with 1/2tsp each (salt, chilli powder, ginger-garlic paste)

In zone 3, add 2 cups finely chopped spinach, 1 chopped green chilli, 1/2tsp salt, 1/2 cup cooked dal

Close, fix weight and switch on the stove. Cook on high for 2 whistles or 5 minutes, whichever comes first. Switch off stove. Release pressure.
Remove beans. Mix well. Serve as dry curry.
Remove tomato. Mash with 1/2 cup water. Mix in potatoes. Serve as gravy.
Remove dal and spinach. Mash with 1/4 cup water. Serve as gravy.

Tip

Can use vegetables, curry pastes of your choice.

LESSON 10: STARCHES

No-water Cooking

No-water Mushroom Biryani

Prep.: Mix 4 cups chopped mushroom, 1/2 cup caramelized onion, 1/4 cup yogurt, 2 slit green chillies, 1tbsp each (garam masala, mint), 1tsp salt. Soak 1 cup basmati rice in water for 30 minutes. Drain.

In a 2L Pressure Baker, layer as below:
Layer 1: 2tbsp ghee
Layer 2: 1 cup chopped tomatoes
Layer 3: 2 cups mushroom
Layer 4: Soaked rice
Layer 5: 2 cups mushroom

Close, fix weight and switch on the stove. Cook on high for 4 whistles or 10 minutes, whichever comes first. Switch off stove. Let pressure settle. Open, mix everything. Fluff up and serve.

Tips

- 1 cup rice needs around 400g mushroom to cook well.
- Ensure top layer of rice is completely covered to avoid drying out.

LESSON 11: LENTILS

Dal

Prep.: Soak 1 cup tuvar dal for 2 hours. Drain.

In a 2L Pressure Baker, layer as below:
Layer 1: 2tbsp ghee
Layer 2: 1/4 cup water
Layer 3: Dal, 1/4tsp turmeric powder

Close, fix weight and switch on the stove. Cook on high for 2 whistles or 5 minutes, whichever comes first. Switch off stove. Let pressure settle. Open, mix everything. Mash if needed.

Tips

- Can use masoor/moong/chana dal.
- Ensure dal doubles in weight after soaking.
- If undercooked, cook for another whistle.

LESSON 12: COLD-PRESSURE FRYING

Bottled Tadka

In a 2L Pressure Baker, add 1 cup refined oil, 1/4 cup each dal (split urad, chana).
Close, fix weight and switch on stove. Cook on high for 3 minutes. Switch off.
Release pressure. Add 1/4 cup each (mustard or cumin, broken dry red chillies). Close. Let cool and bottle.

LESSON 13: BUTTER INTO GHEE

Controlled Evaporation

In a 2L Pressure Baker, add 250g butter.
Close, fix weight and cook on high. Note time gap between the whistles.
Switch off once the gap doubles or there is no whistle for over 15 seconds.
Release pressure. Filter. Bottle when cool to touch.

Tips

- Do not use home-made butter till you understand the technique.
- Do not use more than 250g butter.
- Watch out for the crackling sound which indicates ghee is ready.

LESSON 14: SUGAR SYRUP HACK

Rava Burfi

Prep.: In a greased bowl, add 130g double-roasted rava.

In a 2L Pressure Baker, add 200g sugar, 60g water. Mix well.
Close, fix weight and cook on high for 4 whistles. Release pressure. Pour sugar syrup over rava. Mix well. Let set.

Tips

- Increase whistles to make a stronger syrup.
- Ensure sugar is not wet when measured.
- Weigh all ingredients.

LESSON 15: SCALING-UP

Pressure Bake with Heavily Spiced Curry Paste and Dilute

Kuruma for 8 adults

Prep.: Blend 20 cashewnuts, 10 chopped green chillies, 1.5tsp each (salt, garam masala powder) 1tsp oil, 1/2 cup water to a thick paste. Add to an inner vessel.

In a 2L Pressure Baker, layer as below:
Layer 1: 1/4 cup water, 1tbsp ghee
Layer 2: 1 cup each chopped small (potato, beans, carrot)
Layer 3: PIP – Spice paste (see prep.). Fit in 4 well-washed eggs over the vegetables (optional)

Close, fix weight and switch on the stove. Cook on high for 3 whistles or 5 minutes, whichever comes first. Switch off stove. Release pressure by gently lifting the weight. Open. Remove eggs. Mix spice paste with vegetables. Mix in 1 cup each (milk/coconut milk, hot water). Let eggs cool. Peel and halve. Add to gravy.

LESSON 16: STAPLES

Recipes for ingredients that are used in almost all OPOS dishes can be made and stored for frequent use

OPOS Ginger-garlic Paste*

In a 2L Pressure Baker, layer as below:
Layer 1: 4tbsp oil
Layer 2: 1 cup each (crushed garlic cloves, chopped ginger) arranged side by side

Cook on high for 4 to 5 whistles. Release pressure. Blend to a paste.

---

* Unless otherwise mentioned in recipes, ginger-garlic paste is OPOS ginger-garlic paste.

Tips

- Use in place of ginger-garlic in curries.
- Can mix into curries even after cooking.
- Can refrigerate for weeks or freeze for months.
- Can add 1/4tsp turmeric powder or 1/2tsp vinegar.

Ghee

For recipe, see p. 27.

Caramelized Onions

In a 2L Pressure Baker, layer as below:
Layer 1: 3tbsp oil
Layer 2: 2 cups chopped onions

Cook on high for 4 to 5 minutes or till you smell caramelization. Release pressure. Mix everything.

Tips

- Not caramelized? Chop smaller or cook longer.
- Burnt? Add more oil or chop bigger.
- Caramelization time depends upon the moisture content of the onion.
- Can cook in batches if scaling-up.

Caramelized Tomatoes

In a 2L Pressure Baker, layer as below:
Layer 1: 3tbsp oil
Layer 2: 250g chopped deseeded tomatoes

Cook on high for 4 to 6 minutes. Release pressure.

Tips

- Cook longer for deeper caramelization.
- Caramelization depends on the water content of tomatoes.
- Can cook in batches if scaling-up.

Dals

Prep.: Soak 1/2 cup moong/tuvar dal in water for 1hour. Drain.

In a 2L Pressure Baker, add 1/2 cup water, 1tsp oil, dal. Cook on high for 3 whistles or 4 minutes. Let pressure settle. Reduce water to 1/4 cup for grainy dal and minimize spewing.

Tadka

North Indian Tadka

In a 2L Pressure Baker, add 1 cup oil.
Cook on high for 3 minutes. Release pressure. Mix in 1/2 cup cumin seeds, 1/4 cup red chillies, 1tbsp asafoetida.

Mughlai Tadka

In a 2L Pressure Baker, add 1 cup oil.
Cook on high for 3 minutes. Release pressure. Mix in 3 bay leaves, 1-inch cinnamon, 3 cloves, 1 star anise, 2 each (mace, crushed green cardamom, black cardamom), 1tbsp fennel seeds.

South Indian Tadka with Lentils

In a 2L Pressure Baker, add 1 cup oil. Cook on high for 3.30 minutes. Release pressure. Mix in 1/4 cup each (mustard seeds, lentils), 3tbsp urad dal, 1tbsp chana dal, broken red chillies, curry leaves, 1tsp solid asafoetida.

OPOS Tamarind Paste**

In a 2L Pressure Baker, layer as below:
Layer 1: 250g cleaned and deseeded tamarind
Layer 2: Water to cover the 1.5 cups tamarind (cover the tamarind completely). Cook on high for 4 whistles or 5 minutes. Let pressure settle and cool. Mash and filter if needed. Bottle and store.

Tips

- Always use dry spoons and treat it like a pickle.
- Refrigerate or freeze for longer shelf life.

Coconut–Cumin–Chilli Paste (CCC Paste)

Blend 1 cup grated/chopped coconut, 3 green chillies, 1tsp oil, 1/4tsp salt, 2tsp cumin (optional) with 1/4 cup water to a thick paste.

Tip

Omit green chillies and cumin to make a plain coconut paste.

Spiced Lentil Powder (OPOS Podi)

Blend 1/4 cup roasted gram, 2 dry red chillies, 1/4tsp each (cumin, salt) into a coarse/fine powder.

Replace/Supplement:

- Roasted gram dal with any roasted/fried lentils.
- Red chilli with pepper.
- Gram dal with dry coconut/curry leaves/sun-dried vegetables/ dried seafood.

** Unless otherwise mentioned in recipes, tamarind paste is OPOS tamarind paste.

- Cumin with your favourite spices.

Tips

- Can be used as a cooked dal substitute in curries/stews.
- Stores well for months.
- Roasted tuvar/chana/moong/urad dals are commonly used.

North Indian Mother Sauce (Curry Base)

In a 2L Pressure Baker, layer as below:
Layer 1: 1/4 cup oil
Layer 2: 250g each chopped (onion, deseeded tomato) in bull's-eye method
Layer 3: 1tbsp ginger-garlic paste, 1tsp Kashmiri chilli powder

Cook on high for 5 minutes. Release pressure. Mix well in retained heat.

Tips

- Spice powders are optional.
- Blend for a smoother texture.
- Can be used instead of chopped onion and tomato in recipes.
- Add as top layer to any vegetable/legumes/meat.
- Can be mixed in after cooking.

PREVENTION OF BURNING

Buffer layer

If you are new to OPOS, please repeat these dishes as many times as needed until you are comfortable with the techniques. Only then should you think about scaling up.
To prevent burning, keep these tips in mind:

- In OPOS, most dishes are cooked in high heat for a short period of time, hence there is a possibility of burning, if not done right. To mitigate this, a buffer, mostly water/oil, is used as Layer 1.
- If the recipes require buttermilk/coconut milk/milk as a buffer layer, ensure they are in diluted form.

  1:10 = yogurt: water = buttermilk ratio

  1:4 = milk/coconut milk: water = milk/coconut milk ratio
- The water measures mentioned in the recipes are for fresh vegetables. If vegetables are dry/old/refrigerated/not tender, an extra bit of water needs to be added to the buffer layer. (For instance, refrigerated cut vegetables dry out as the refrigerator acts as a dehydrator. These need extra water in Layer 1.)
- Whenever water is mentioned, it is water at room temperature.
- It is recommended to soak and drain the legumes/lentils and discard the soaked/drained water before cooking them.
- Understand and get comfortable with recipes that use water in Layer 1 before attempting no-water recipes.

Layering done right

- Always spread the ingredients evenly.
- Whenever a recipe calls for layering of spice powders/pastes, ensure they are layered over the vegetables/starches/meat, as a top layer. This will prevent them from seeping down/touching the Pressure Baker base and burning. If the spice pastes turn out to be runny, place a small cup on the top layer and add the spice paste to it.
- Whenever a recipe calls for retained heat cooking, for e.g., in the Kesari (p. 202) or Upma (p. 164) recipes, ensure the ingredients are swiftly mixed in and the Pressure Baker is closed immediately to ensure maximum heat retention.

Avoiding overcooking and undercooking

- When a recipe calls for (X) whistles or (Y) minutes, whichever comes first is considered.
- If vegetables are overcooked, try the following steps to avoid it the next time:
  - Reduce the cooking time (by cooking them for one whistle less).
  - Cut them thicker.
  - Release pressure after cooking if you had let pressure settle.
- If vegetables are undercooked, try the following suggestions:
  - Increase the cooking time (by cooking them for one whistle more) and release pressure.
  - Cut them thinner.
  - Mix and keep closed in the retained heat, after releasing pressure.

Is something burning?

At the faintest smell of burning or sight of white smoke, turn the heat source off and release pressure, if any. Transfer the contents. Do not scrape/consume the black/charred bits. This will not affect the flavour of the output.

SECTION III
BEGINNER'S LUCK

All-time Favourites

To get you started, these recipes are our tried-and-tested best

GUTTI VANKAYA KURA

Telugu Stuffed Brinjal

Prep.: Mix 1/4 cup puliyogare powder and 1/4tsp salt. Slit 250g brinjal into four so that they remain joined at the base. Stuff spice mix tightly into brinjal. Wipe brinjal surface clean.

In a 2L Pressure Baker, layer as below:
Layer 1: 2tbsp each (oil, water)
Layer 2: Stuffed brinjal
Cook on high heat for 3 whistles or 5 minutes. Release pressure.

Replace/Supplement:

- Spice mix for stuffing with thengai molagapodi (spiced roasted coconut powder)/paruppu podi (p. 188).
- Can add tamarind paste, ginger-garlic paste, sambar powder in stuffing.

Tips

- Choose small, baby brinjal. Thick ones take longer to cook.
- Cook longer for roasted effect.
- Tender brinjals cook faster. Some cook in 2 whistles.

HOTEL SARAVANA BHAVAN (HSB) KURUMA

South Indian Mixed Vegetable Stew

Prep.: Spiced coconut paste: Blend 1/4 cup chopped coconut, 1tbsp cashews, 1tsp each (ginger-garlic paste, salt), 1/2tsp garam masala powder, 2 green chillies, a pinch of turmeric powder, 1tsp oil, 2tbsp water to a thick paste.

In a 2L Pressure Baker, layer as below:
Layer 1: 1/4 cup water
Layer 2: 1/2 cup each chopped (carrot, beans, potato)
Layer 3: Spiced coconut paste
Layer 4: 1/2 cup green peas in an inner vessel

Cook on high for 3 whistles or 5 minutes. Release pressure. Mix everything with 1/2 cup coconut milk and serve.

Replace/Supplement:

- Water with vegetable stock.
- Garam masala powder with any favourite spice powder.
- Cashews with roasted gram dal.

Tips

- Can dilute as per the needed consistency.
- Can also add caramelized (onion/tomato).

PANEER BUTTER MASALA

North Indian Cottage Cheese Creamy Curry

Prep.: Mix in 1 cup paneer cubes with 1/4tsp each (salt, chilli powder, garam masala powder, dry fenugreek leaves), a pinch of turmeric powder.

In a 2L Pressure Baker, layer as below:
Layer 1: 3tbsp butter
Layer 2: 1 cup onion petals, 125g small whole tomatoes, 1 green chilli, 1 garlic clove, 2tsp chopped ginger, 10 cashews
Layer 3: PIP – 1 cup spiced paneer

Cook on high for 3 whistles or 5 minutes. Release pressure. Remove PIP. Blend the base gravy with 1/4 cup cream. Mix in the spiced paneer. Dilute with water/stock as desired.

Replace/Supplement:

- Butter with oil/ghee.
- Garam masala with favourite spice mix.
- Onion petals with shallots.
- Paneer with tofu/soya.
- Spiced paneer with plain paneer.

Tip

Replace paneer with vegetables/meats for more variations.

BUTTER CHICKEN

Chicken in Rich, Creamy Buttery Curry

Prep.: Mix 500g chicken, 1tbsp each (Kashmiri chilli powder, ginger-garlic paste), 1tsp each (dry fenugreek leaves, cumin powder, salt), 1/2tsp garam masala powder, 1/4tsp turmeric powder.

In a 2L Pressure Baker, layer as below:
Layer 1: 1/4 cup butter
Layer 2: Spiced chicken
Layer 3: 3 large, scooped tomatoes filled with 2tbsp almond powder, 1tsp sugar

Cook on high for 8 whistles or 6 minutes. Let pressure settle. Remove the chicken and blend the base with 1/2 cup cream, 1 tbsp butter. Mix in chicken and serve.

Replace/Supplement:

- Chicken with baby potatoes/mushrooms (5 whistles).
- Spice powders with any ready-made spice mix.

Tips

- Can add more cream or butter for a richer and creamier version.
- Wipe spice paste from the surface (of the chicken) touching the base of the cooker.
- Cook for longer and allow pressure to settle if using bigger chunks.

WHOLE CHICKEN ROAST

Prep.: Pat dry whole chicken (1,200g approximately). Make multiple deep cuts. Mix 2 tbsp chilli powder, 1 tbsp each (ginger-garlic paste, salt), 2 tsp garam masala powder, 1 tbsp oil to paste. Apply the paste all over the chicken except the bottom.

In a 2L Pressure Baker, layer as below:
Layer 1: 1/4 cup oil
Layer 2: Marinated whole chicken

Cook on high for 15 whistles or 10 minutes. Let pressure settle. Open and serve.

Replace/Supplement:

- Chicken with whole quail (5 whistles).
- Chilli powder with chicken masala/any favourite spice mix.

Tips

- Ensure spice paste does not touch the cooker base.
- Make multiple deep slits so that the chicken cooks evenly inside.
- Apply the spice paste into the slits for a much better taste.
- Can marinate for deeper flavour.

CHICKEN BIRYANI

Chicken–Rice Casserole

Prep.: Mix 500g chicken chopped small, 1 cup yogurt, 1/4 cup each chopped (coriander, mint leaves), 3tbsp caramelized onion, 1tbsp ginger-garlic paste, 2tsp biryani masala, 1/2tsp salt, 1tsp garam masala powder, 1 slit chilli. Soak 1 cup basmati rice in water for 30 minutes. Drain.

In a 2L Pressure Baker, layer as below:
Layer 1: 1/4 cup water, 1tbsp ghee
Layer 2: 1/2 cup chopped tomato
Layer 3: Half of the spiced chicken to cover the base
Layer 4: Rice
Layer 5: Remaining spiced chicken to cover the rice completely

Cook on high for 5 whistles or 10 minutes. Let pressure settle. Open and fluff up.

Replace/Supplement:

- Chicken with fish/prawns.
- Biryani masala with garam masala powder.
- Ghee with your favourite oil.
- Onion with shallots.
- Yogurt with coconut milk.

Tips

- Use bite-sized chicken pieces.
- Vegetarians can use mushroom/soya chunks/paneer in place of chicken.
- Can marinate chicken overnight.
- Ensure the top layer of rice is completely covered.

PASTA ARRABBIATA

Pasta in Spicy Tomato Sauce

In a 2L Pressure Baker, layer as below:
Layer 1: 1tbsp oil
Layer 2: 200g sliced tomatoes to cover the base
Layer 3: 1 cup Indian macaroni
Layer 4: 1tsp Italian seasoning, 1/2tsp each (paprika, salt)
Layer 5: 1/2 cup sliced tomato to cover the pasta completely

Cook on high for 4 whistles or 6 minutes. Release pressure. Mix everything and keep closed for 5 minutes.

Replace/Supplement:

- Macaroni with other varieties of pasta.
- Tomato with mushroom or other watery vegetables.
- Chilli powder with your favourite spice mix.
- Oil with butter.

Tips

- Indian pasta cooks faster than Western brands.
- Harder pastas need to be washed and used or soaked briefly and used.
- If undercooked, soak/cook longer/do not release pressure.
- Pasta needs over thrice its volume of watery vegetables to cook well.

MYSORE PAK

Gram flour Fudge

In a 2L Pressure Baker, add 200g sugar, 1/4 cup water, 1tbsp ghee. Mix well. Cook on high for 3 whistles or 3 minutes. Release pressure. Mix in 100g well-roasted and sieved gram flour (besan), 20g milk powder, 3tbsp ghee. Pour in a greased container, let sit and cut into squares while the mixture is warm.

Replace/Supplement:

- Gram flour with other roasted seed/nut flours/sattu flour (made of ground pulses and cereals).
- Besan with roasted chickpeas (kabuli chana) freshly blended to a flour.

Tips

- Vary cooking time to vary texture.
- Use a weighing scale to measure ingredients. Cup measures can be tricky.
- Three whistles give a soft fudge; 4 to 5 whistles give a firm one.
- Can mix in 1/2tsp baking powder for a porous texture.
- Can add more ghee for softer fudge.
- Roast gram flour multiple times on low heat. Roast, let cool and roast again. Repeat until it loses the raw taste. There would be a mild colour change with the roasting of the flour.
- Can use a mixture of flours for an interesting flavour.
- Can layer different coloured fudges to make a multilayer cake.
- Can add cardamom powder or other sweet spices for flavour.
- The cooker needs to be washed immediately after cooking. If you let it dry, the syrup solidifies and makes cleaning tough. Add water and soak/cook for a whistle to clean it easily.

COLD PRESSURE-FRIED FRENCH FRIES

In a 2L Pressure Baker, add 1 cup oil, 250g frozen potato french fries.
Cook on high for 9 minutes. Release pressure. Drain oil.
Add a pinch of salt and a pinch of pepper and toss.

Replace/Supplement:

- Potato fries with frozen sweet potato sticks.
- Pepper with paprika/favourite seasoning.

Tips

- Cooking time varies marginally with the thickness of potato sticks. Thinner sticks cook faster.
- Do not thaw. Use directly from the freezer.

CARROT HALWA

Carrot Fudge

In a 2L Pressure Baker, layer as below:
Layer 1: 2tbsp water, 1tbsp ghee
Layer 2: 2 cups grated carrots
Layer 3: 1/2 cup sugar, 1/4tsp cardamom powder

Cook on high for 10 whistles or 5 minutes. Release pressure. Mix in 1/4 cup khoya and serve.

Replace/Supplement:

- Carrot with beetroot/winter melon/squash.
- Cardamom with sweet spices.
- Sugar with jaggery/favourite sweeteners.
- Khoya with milk powder/paneer/condensed milk.
- Can add roasted nuts.

Tips

- Can serve hot/cold.
- The timing/whistles depend on the moisture content of carrots.
- Go by your nose. Wait for a faint burnt smell.
- Can reduce sugar.

SECTION IV
MONDAY TO SUNDAY

What is Modular Cooking?

How do you introduce variety into your weeknight meals with minimal fuss? OPOS it!

OPOS uses the Modular Cooking concept to translate one recipe into multiple cuisines.

The idea of using modules or building blocks exist in every field. In home design, you set up a modular kitchen or bedroom by just invoking prebuilt units. In software, you have a set of subroutines you can invoke to do often repeated steps.

In OPOS, we build complex recipes from the ground up, across cuisines, by just using the appropriate modules. Just one module can change the parentage of the recipe. We can easily jump cuisines or create new fusion cuisines by just adding/deleting modules.

Here's how it works. Vegetables/meats/seafood and starches are common to all cuisines. Only the spices/additives and cooking technique varies. All OPOS recipes are designed so that the core building blocks can be varied, giving rise to a multitude of recipes across cuisines, from a core theme.

Let's take an example:

Layer 1: 2tbsp water
Layer 2: 2 cup chopped vegetables
Layer 3: 1/4tsp each (salt, pepper)
Cook on high for 2 whistles. Release pressure. Mix all.

This is a universal recipe. It can fit into any cuisine. Now, let's add a flavouring module as Layer 4, say 1/2tsp (garam masala/Bengali panch phoron/Maharashtrian goda masala/Tamil sambar powder). You can now see the recipe jumping cuisines. By adding more modules, you can convert the same recipe into a full meal/stew/soup/dessert from any cuisine. Each layer can be a simple ingredient or a complex module.

Each cuisine interprets these universal themes with its favourite ingredients and cooking techniques, to generate its own recipes.

Both our Monday to Sunday and What's In Your Fridge sections have been designed on these principles of modular cooking. Enjoy!

Soup Module

SOUPS

Base: Vegetables, Meat, Lentils
Flavouring: Stock (p. 53-54), Herbs, Spices
Additives: Cooked Grains, Processed Grains, Eggs, Cheese
Garnish: Croutons, Toasted Nuts/Seeds, Spring Onion, Grated Ginger, Fried Onion, Cilantro

Monday: Pureed Vegetable Soup

In a 2L Pressure Baker, layer as below:
Layer 1: 2tbsp each (butter, water)
Layer 2: 2 cups each chopped vegetables (carrot, potato, squash, mushroom, broccoli, cauliflower)
Layer 3: 1/2tsp salt

Cook on high for 3 whistles or 4 minutes. Release pressure. Blend with 1tbsp butter, 1tsp pepper, 1 cup water/stock.

Tuesday: Russian Borscht

In a 2L Pressure Baker, layer as below:
Layer 1: 2tbsp butter, 1tbsp water
Layer 2: 1 each (crushed garlic clove, bay leaf)
Layer 3: 1 cup grated beetroot
Layer 4: 1/2 cup each chopped (carrot, potato)
Layer 5: 1tbsp each (caramelized onion, tomato ketchup)
Layer 6: 1/2 cup canned beans/sprouts, 1/2tsp salt

Cook on high for 2 whistles or 5 minutes. Release pressure. Mix in 1tsp vinegar/lemon juice, 2 cups hot stock, 1/4 cup finely chopped capsicum, 1tbsp chopped dill/cilantro.

Wednesday: Dal Shorba (Indian Lentil Soup)

Prep.: Soak 1/2 cup split moong/masoor/tuvar dal for 3 hours. Drain.

In a 2L Pressure Baker, layer as below:
Layer 1: 1/4 cup water, 2tbsp ghee
Layer 2: Dal, a pinch of asafoetida, 1tsp ginger-garlic paste
Layer 3: PIP – 1 cup fresh green peas

Cook on high for 4 whistles or 5 minutes. Release pressure. Blend everything with 1/2tsp each (salt, pepper), 2 cups water/stock.

Thursday: Thai Tom Yum Soup

Prep.: Crush 1tbsp each chopped (lemongrass, galangal, kaffir lime leaves), 2 garlic cloves (substitute: cilantro roots, ginger, lemon zest).

In a 2L Pressure Baker, add 1 cup water/stock, crushed paste, 1 slit green chilli, 250g chopped prawns/seafood, 1tbsp each caramelized (tomato, onion), 1 cup chopped mushroom, 1/2tsp each (fish sauce, sugar), 1/4tsp salt.

Cook on high for 3 whistles or 5 minutes. Release pressure. Mix in 1tsp lemon juice, 1/4 cup chopped cilantro. For a creamier version, mix in 1/4 cup milk/coconut milk.

Friday: Gazpacho (Spanish Cold Soup)

Blend 1 cup each (chopped cucumber/tomato/capsicum/zucchini/ watermelon, stock/water), 1 bread slice, 1 garlic clove/shallot, 1tbsp oil, 1/2tsp each (salt, pepper, cumin), 1tsp vinegar.

Saturday: Minestrone (Italian Pasta Soup)

In a 2L Pressure Baker, add 1tbsp olive oil, 1/2 cup each (macaroni, canned beans or sprouts, carrot cut big, mushroom or favourite vegetable mix), 1tbsp caramelized onion, 1 cup chopped tomato, 1/2tsp each (salt, chilli flakes) 1tsp pizza seasoning/oregano. Cover with water/stock.

Cook on high for 3 whistles or 6 minutes. Let pressure settle. Mix in 1tbsp grated cheese, 1/2tsp lemon juice.

Sunday: Thukpa (Tibetan Noodle Soup)

In a 2L Pressure Baker, add 1tbsp butter, 1/2 cup crushed noodles, 1/2 cup each (carrot, cabbage cut to stamp-size, mushroom), 1tsp each (ginger-garlic paste, soy sauce), 1 slit green chilli, 1/2tsp each (salt, pepper, chilli flakes). Cover with water/stock.

Cook on high for 3 whistles. Release pressure. Mix in 1tbsp cilantro.

Tips

- Mix 1 beaten egg into hot soup to make it an egg drop soup.
- Mix in soy sauce, vinegar and chilli paste to convert it into hot and sour soup.
- Mix 1/4 cup cooked rice/grains to make it carb-rich.
- Mix in pesto/chutney other sauces for a burst of flavour.
- Mix in chopped hard-boiled egg/cheese/paneer/sausage/flaked meats/canned fish to make it protein rich.
- Mix in 1/2 cup cream to make it a 'Cream of ___' soup.
- Mix in butter to make it fat rich.

Making vegetable stock:

In a 2L Pressure Baker, add 1/2 cup each chopped (onion, carrot), 1 bay leaf, 1tsp each (peppercorn, ginger-garlic paste). Add 2 cups water.

Cook on high for 5 whistles or 5 minutes. Let pressure settle. Filter and store. Dilute with more water while using.

Making chicken/fish stock:

In a 2L Pressure Baker, add 500g chicken with bones/fish heads, 1/2 cup each chopped (onion, carrot), 2 garlic cloves, 1 bay leaf. Cover with water.

Cook on high for 6 whistles or 7 minutes. Let pressure settle. Skim off the top layer. Filter and bottle. Flake chicken/fish and mix meat into salads. Discard vegetables.

Making instant stock:

Mix 1tbsp stock powder with 2 cups water.

RASAM

Base: Stock (p. 53-54)
Flavouring: Spices, Bottled Tadka (p. 26)
Additives: Cilantro, Jaggery

Monday: Paruppu Rasam

Prep.: Soak 1/4 cup dal each (moong, tuvar, masoor, horse gram) in water for 4 hours. Drain.

In a 2L Pressure Baker, add 1/2 cup water, dal, 1tsp rasam powder, 1/2tsp salt, 1/4tsp each (turmeric powder, asafoetida).

Cook on high for 6 whistles or 6 minutes. Let pressure settle. Mash dal. Strain. Mix in 2 cups liquid (see p. 52), 1tsp bottled tadka.

Tuesday: Chettinad Chicken Rasam

In a 2L Pressure Baker, add 1 cup each (water, chicken with bones) 1 crushed garlic clove, 1/4 cup each chopped (shallots, tomato), 1tsp rasam powder, 1/2tsp salt, 1/4tsp each (turmeric powder, pepper).

Cook on high for 5 whistles or 6 minutes. Let pressure settle. Strain. Mix in 2 cups liquid (see p. 52), 1 tsp bottled tadka.

Wednesday: Vegetable Rasam

In a 2L Pressure Baker, add 1 cup each (water/stock, finely chopped vegetables [carrot/beetroot/drumsticks], 1 tsp rasam powder, 1/2 tsp salt.

Cook on high for 6 whistles or 5 minutes. Let pressure settle. Strain. Mix in 2 cups liquid (see p. 52), 1 tsp bottled tadka.

Thursday: Nandu Rasam (Crab Rasam)

In a 2L Pressure Baker, add 1 cup each (water, cleaned and chopped crab), 1 crushed garlic clove, 1/4 cup each chopped (shallots, tomato), 1 tsp rasam powder, 1/2 tsp salt.

Cook on high for 10 whistles or 5 minutes. Let pressure settle. Strain. Mix in 2 cups liquid (see p. 52), 1 tsp bottled tadka.

Friday: Spice-based Rasam

In a 2L Pressure Baker, add 1 cup water, 1/4 cup chopped ginger/garlic, 1 tsp rasam powder, 1/2 tsp each (salt, crushed [pepper, cumin]).

Cook on high for 10 whistles or 5 minutes. Let pressure settle. Strain. Mix in 2 cups liquid (see p. 52), 1 tsp bottled tadka.

Saturday: Fruit-based Rasam

In a 2L Pressure Baker, add 1 cup each (water, chopped fruit [tomato/mango/pineapple]), 1 tsp rasam powder, 1/2 tsp salt, 1/4 tsp turmeric powder.

Cook on high for 10 whistles or 5 minutes. Let pressure settle. Strain. Mix in 2 cups liquid (see p. 52), 1 tsp bottled tadka.

Sunday: Herb-based Rasam

In a 2L Pressure Baker, add 1 cup water, 2 cups chopped herbs (mint/
curry leaves/fenugreek leaves/lemongrass), 1tsp rasam powder, 1/2tsp
salt, 1/4tsp turmeric powder.

Cook on high for 10 whistles or 5 minutes. Let pressure settle. Strain.
Mix in 2 cups liquid (see below), 1tsp bottled tadka.

Liquids:

Vegetable/meat stock, lentil stock, tamarind water, thin coconut milk,
thin buttermilk.

Rasam powder:

Roast 1/4 cup coriander seeds, 5 dry red chillies, 1tbsp each (pepper,
cumin), 1/4tsp asafoetida. Blend to a coarse powder.

Common tadka:

Mustard seeds, cumin seeds, dry red chilli in ghee.

Tips

- Serve as a soup with papad.
- Mix in pepper powder, lemon juice for punch.
- Mix in a coarse paste of aromatics (ginger, garlic, herbs, chillies)
  after cooking for a flavour burst.
- Souring agent is optional in most rasams, though tamarind paste
  is commonly used.
- Mix in the strained stuff with other gravies.

Salads Module

KANNADIGA KOSAMBARI (SOAKED LENTIL SALAD)

Base: Soaked Chana/Moong Dal
Flavouring: Bottled Tadka (p. 26), Herbs
Additives: Salad Vegetables, Fruits, Nuts, Dressing, Grain Flakes, Puffed Grains, Coconut, Lemon Juice

Monday: Classic Kannadiga Kosambari

Soak 1/4 cup split moong dal for 2 hours. Drain. Mix in 1/4 cup grated coconut, 1 chopped green chilli, 1tbsp chopped cilantro, 1/4tsp salt, 1tsp lemon juice.

Tuesday: Cucumber Kosambari

Soak 1/4 cup split moong dal for 2 hours. Drain. Mix in 1/4 cup each (grated coconut, chopped cucumber), 1 chopped green chilli, 1/4tsp salt, 1tsp lemon juice.

Wednesday: Chana Dal Kosambari

Soak 1/4 cup split chana dal overnight. Drain. Mix in 1/4 cup each (grated coconut, chopped cucumber, grated carrot), 1 chopped green chilli, 1/4tsp salt, 1tsp lemon juice.

Thursday: Sprouted Kosambari

Take 1 cup mixed sprouts. Mix in 1/4 cup grated coconut, 1 chopped green chilli, 1/4tsp salt, 1tsp lemon juice.

Friday: Andhra Vada Pappu

Soak 1/4 cup split moong dal for 2 hours. Drain. Mix in 1/4 cup grated coconut, 1tbsp grated raw mango, 1 chopped green chilli, 1/4tsp salt, 1tsp lemon juice.

Saturday: Tamil Carrot Kosumalli

Soak 1/4 cup split moong dal for 2 hours. Drain. Mix in 1/4 cup each grated (coconut, carrot), 1 chopped green chilli, 1/4tsp salt, 1tsp lemon juice, 1tsp bottled tadka.

Sunday: Dalimbe Kosambari

Soak 1/4 cup split moong dal for 2 hours. Drain. Mix in 1/4 cup grated coconut, 1/4 cup each (sweet corn, pomegranate pearls), 1 chopped green chilli, 1/2tsp salt, 1tsp lemon juice.

SALADS

Base: Vegetables, Fruits, Meats/Eggs
Flavouring: Herbs, Spices, Salad Dressing (p. 60)
Additives: Paneer, Chopped Bread, Cheese, Croutons, Spring Onion, Lemon Zest
Garnish: Croutons, Chopped Nuts, Bhujia/Sev

Monday: Raw Vegetable Salad

Mix 1/2 cup each chopped (onion, tomato, cucumber, lettuce), 1/2tsp each (pepper, salt), 2tbsp salad dressing.

Tuesday: Cooked Vegetable Salad

In a 2L Pressure Baker, layer as below:
Layer 1: 1tbsp each (oil, water)
Layer 2: 2 cups chopped vegetables
Layer 3: 1/4tsp salt

Cook on high for 3 whistles or 4 minutes. Release pressure. Mix everything with 1tsp pepper, 1/4 cup each chopped (onion, tomato, lettuce), 2tbsp salad dressing.

Wednesday: Fruit Salad

Mix 2 cups chopped fruits (apple, peach, pear, pineapple, banana, mango, seedless grapes), 1/4 cup nuts with 2tbsp salad dressing. Or mix in chocolate sauce/condensed milk for a sweet version.

Thursday: Sprouts/Bean Salad

In a 2L Pressure Baker, layer as below:
Layer 1: 1/4 cup water
Layer 2: 2 cups sprouts
Layer 3: 1/4tsp salt

Cook on high for 4 whistles or 5 minutes. Release pressure. Mix everything with 1tsp pepper, 1/2 cup each chopped (onion, tomato, cucumber), 2tbsp salad dressing.

Friday: Egg Salad

In a 2L Pressure Baker, add 1/2 cup water, 6 well-washed eggs. Cook on high for 1 whistle or 4 minutes. Let pressure settle. Peel and chop eggs. Mix everything with 1tsp pepper, 1/4tsp salt, 1/2 cup each chopped (onion, tomato, cucumber), 2tbsp salad dressing.

Saturday: Chicken Salad

In a 2L Pressure Baker, layer as below:
Layer 1: 1tbsp oil
Layer 2: 250g boneless chicken chopped small
Layer 3: 1/4tsp salt

Cook on high for 4 whistles or 5 minutes. Release pressure. Mix everything with 1tsp pepper, 1/2 cup each chopped (onion, tomato, cucumber), 2tbsp salad dressing.

Sunday: Bread Salad

Mix 1/2 cup chopped bread/flatbread, 1/2 cup each chopped (onion, tomato, cucumber, lettuce), 1/2tsp each (pepper, salt), 2tbsp salad dressing.

Salad dressings:

Hung yogurt, mayonnaise, bottled tadka, lemon juice, tomato sauce, mustard sauce, ready-made salad dressings or any combination of these.

Tips

In all the above salads, mix in:

- Chopped bread/cooked rice/pasta/cooked grains/sweet corn for a carb-rich salad.
- Paneer/cheese/flaked meats/fish/sausages for a protein-rich salad.
- Virgin olive oil/coconut oil for a fat rich-salad.

TAMIL SUNDAL (CHANA CHAAT/SPICED LEGUMES)

Base: Legumes
Flavouring: Bottled Tadka (p. 26)
Additives: Coconut, Mango, Herbs

Monday: Classic Sundal

Prep.: Soak 1/2 cup split chana dal in water for 2 hours. Drain.

In a 2L Pressure Baker, add 1/4 cup water, 2 chopped green chillies, dal, 1/2tsp salt.

Cook on high for 4 whistles or 5 minutes. Let pressure settle. Mix in 1/4 cup grated coconut, 1tbsp bottled tadka.

Tuesday: Fresh Legume/Sprouts Sundal

Prep.: Take 2 cups fresh legumes (green peas, mixed sprouts, etc.)/ sweet corn.

In a 2L Pressure Baker, layer as below:
Layer 1: 1/4 cup water
Layer 2: 2 cups legumes, 2 chopped green chillies, 1/2tsp salt

Cook on high for 3 whistles or 5 minutes. Let pressure settle. Drain excess water, if any. Mix in 1/4 cup grated coconut, 1tbsp bottled tadka.

Wednesday: Small Legume Sundal

Prep.: Soak 1/2 cup whole legumes (fenugreek/horse gram/urad dal/ moong dal/peanuts) overnight. Drain.

In a 2L Pressure Baker, add 1/2 cup water, 2 chopped green chillies, dal.

Cook on high for 5 whistles or 6 minutes. Let pressure settle. Drain excess water, if any. Mix in 1/4 cup grated coconut, 1tbsp bottled tadka.

Thursday: Large Legume Sundal

Prep.: Soak 1/2 cup whole legumes (desi chana/kabuli chana/rajma/ green peas/black-eyed peas) overnight. Drain.

In a 2L Pressure Baker, add 1/2 cup water, 2 chopped green chillies, dal.

Cook on high for 10 whistles or 8 minutes. Let pressure settle. Drain excess water, if any. Mix in 1/4 cup grated coconut, 1tbsp bottled tadka, 1/2tsp salt.

Friday: Beach Sundal

Prep.: Soak 1/2 cup dried green peas in water overnight. Drain.

In a 2L Pressure Baker, layer as below:
Layer 1: 1/4 cup water
Layer 2: Peas, 2 chopped green chillies, 1/2tsp salt

Cook on high for 3 whistles or 5 minutes. Let pressure settle. Drain excess water, if any. Mix in 1tbsp each (grated coconut, bottled tadka, chopped onion, grated carrot).

Saturday: Sweet Sundal

Prep.: Soak 1 cup whole moong dal/split chana dal in water for 3 hours. Drain.

In a 2L Pressure Baker, layer as below:
Layer 1: 1/4 cup water
Layer 2: Dal
Layer 3: PIP – add 1/4 cup jaggery

Cook on high for 3 whistles or 5 minutes. Let pressure settle. Drain excess water, if any. Mix in 1/4 cup grated coconut, 1tbsp bottled tadka.

Sunday: Chana Chaat

Prep.: Soak 1/2 cup desi chickpeas in water overnight. Drain.

In a 2L Pressure Baker, layer as below:
Layer 1: 1/4 cup water
Layer 2: Chickpeas

Cook on high for 8 whistles or 10 minutes. Let pressure settle. Drain excess water, if any. Mix in 1/4 cup each chopped (onion, tomato), 1 chopped green chilli, 1tsp each (bottled tadka, lime juice), 1/2tsp black salt, 1tbsp chopped cilantro.

Common tadka:

Mustard seeds, dry red chilli, split urad dal, curry leaves, asafoetida.

Tip

Soak in salted water for deeper flavour.

CHAAT (NORTH INDIAN STREET FOOD)

Base: Salad Vegetables, Fruits, Puffed Rice, Pooris, Potato
Flavouring: Herbs, Spices, Chutneys (p. 65)
Additives: Sev, Mango, Yogurt, Salad Vegetables

Monday: Fruit Chaat

Mix 2 cups chopped mixed fruits with 1tbsp chutney, 1tsp lemon juice, 1/2tsp each (black salt, chaat masala), 1tsp roasted cumin powder.

Tuesday: Puffed Rice-based Chaat

Mix 2 cups puffed rice with 1/4 cup each finely chopped (onion, tomato, cucumber), 1tbsp each (grated [carrot, beetroot], chutney, chopped cilantro), 1/4 cup sev/bhujia, 1tsp lemon juice.

Wednesday: Legume-based Chaat

In a 2L Pressure Baker, layer as below:
Layer 1: 1/4 cup water
Layer 2: 2 cups sprouts, 1/2tsp chilli powder

Cook on high for 3 whistles or 6 minutes. Release pressure. Mix with 1/4 cup each finely chopped (onion, tomato, cucumber), 2tbsp chutney, 1tbsp each chopped (raw mango, cilantro), 1/2tsp each (black salt, chaat masala, roasted cumin powder), 1 chopped green chilli.

Thursday: Starchy Vegetable-based Chaat

In a 2L Pressure Baker, layer as below:
Layer 1: 1/4 cup oil
Layer 2: 2 cups starchy vegetables chopped to bite size (potato/raw banana/yam/sweet potato)
Layer 3: 1tsp ginger-garlic paste, 1/2tsp chilli powder, a pinch of turmeric powder

Cook on high for 4 whistles or 6 minutes. Release pressure. Drain oil. Mix in 1/4 cup each finely chopped (onion, tomato, cucumber), 2tbsp chutney, 1/4 cup each (sev, pomegranate pearls), 1/2tsp each (black salt, chaat masala, roasted cumin powder), 1 chopped green chilli, 1tbsp chopped cilantro.

Friday: Mixed Vegetable-based Chaat

In a 2L Pressure Baker, layer as below:
Layer 1: 3tbsp butter
Layer 2: 1/2 cup each chopped (onion, tomato) arranged in bull's-eye method
Layer 3: 1 cup chopped mixed vegetables (potato, beans, carrot, beetroot)
Layer 4: PIP – 1 cup mixed delicate vegetables (peas, capsicum, cauliflower)
Layer 5: 1tsp ginger-garlic paste, 1/2tsp each (salt, chilli powder, garam masala powder)

Cook on high for 3 whistles or 5 minutes. Release pressure. Mash and serve with toasted bread/pav.

Saturday: Puffed Poori-based Chaat

Prep.: Spiced water: Mix 1tbsp green chutney, 1/2tsp each (chaat masala, mango [amchur] powder, cumin powder, pepper powder, black salt) with 2 cups water.

Filling:

In a 2L Pressure Baker, layer as below:
Layer 1: 1/4 cup water
Layer 2: 1 cup chopped potato
Layer 3: 1 cup sprouts
Layer 4: 1tsp ginger-garlic paste, 1/2tsp each (salt, chilli powder), a pinch of turmeric powder

Cook on high for 4 whistles or 6 minutes. Release pressure. Mash coarsely. Mix in 1/4 cup finely chopped onion, 2tbsp chutney, 1/2tsp each (black salt, chaat masala, roasted cumin powder), 1 chopped green chilli, 1tbsp chopped cilantro.

Assembly options

- Fill pani poori shells with filling and spiced water.
- Fill pani poori shells with filling. Add chutneys. Cover with sev, chopped cilantro to make it sev pooris.
- Fill pani poori shells with filling. Add chutneys. Cover with sev, chopped cilantro, yogurt to make it dahi pooris.

Sunday: Egg and Starchy Vegetable-based Chaat

In a 2L Pressure Baker, layer as below:
Layer 1: 1/4 cup oil
Layer 2: 2 cups starchy vegetables chopped to bite size (potato/raw banana/yam)
Layer 3: 1tsp ginger-garlic paste, 1/2tsp chilli powder, a pinch of turmeric powder
Layer 4: 3 well-washed eggs

Cook on high for 4 whistles or 6 minutes. Release pressure. Remove eggs. Drain oil. Let eggs cool. Peel and chop eggs. Mix everything with 1/4 cup each finely chopped (onion, tomato, cucumber), 2tbsp chutney, 1/4 cup sev, 1/2tsp each (black salt, chaat masala, roasted cumin powder, pepper, amchur), 1 chopped green chilli, 1tbsp chopped cilantro.

Chutneys for chaat:

Green chutney

Blend 1/2 cup each chopped (cilantro, mint), 2 each (green chillies, garlic cloves), 1/4 cup water, 1/2tsp salt, 1tsp oil.

Sweet and sour chutney:

Mix 1/4 cup jaggery, 3tsp tamarind paste, 1/4tsp each (chilli powder, cumin powder, black salt), 1/4 cup water.

Red chutney

Blend 1/2 cup garlic cloves, 1tsp each (Kashmiri chilli powder, oil), 1/2tsp salt to a paste. Mix in 1/4 cup water.

Dates chutney

Blend 1/2 cup chopped dates, 1tbsp each (tamarind, jaggery), 1/2tsp each (roasted cumin, red chilli powder, dry ginger powder), 1/4tsp salt to a paste with 1/4 cup water.

Tips

- Mix and serve immediately.
- Can add paneer to all chaats above for a protein punch.
- Can add roasted thin poha/sweet corn to all chaats above to add carbs.

Meals Module

NORTH INDIAN KADHAI (SPICED STIR-FRY)

Base: Vegetables, Meat, Seafood
Flavouring: Ginger-garlic Paste (p. 28), Spices, Garam Masala Powder, Herbs
Additives: Nuts, Milk/Cream/Yogurt, Caramelized Onion/Tomato (p. 29)

Monday: Kadhai Mixed Vegetable

In a 2L Pressure Baker, layer as below:
Layer 1: 2tbsp oil
Layer 2: 1 cup onion petals cut to stamp-size
Layer 3: 1/2 cup carrot slices
Layer 4: 1/2 cup each (capsicum cut to stamp-size, cauliflower florets cut to bite size) mixed with 1tsp ginger-garlic paste, 1/2tsp each (salt, Kashmiri chilli powder, garam masala powder)

Cook on high for 2 whistles or 4 minutes. Release pressure. Mix everything.

Tuesday: Kadhai Paneer

In a 2L Pressure Baker, layer as below:
Layer 1: 2tbsp butter
Layer 2: 1/2 cup each (onion petals, deseeded tomato), cut to stamp-size

Layer 3: 1/2 cup capsicum cut to stamp-size and 1 cup paneer cut to bite size mixed with 1tsp ginger-garlic paste, 1/2tsp each (salt, Kashmiri chilli powder, garam masala powder)

Cook on high for 2 whistles or 4 minutes. Release pressure. Mix everything.

Wednesday: Shahi Kadhai Mushroom

In a 2L Pressure Baker, layer as below:
Layer 1: 2tbsp butter
Layer 2: 200g mushrooms with stalk and head separated
Layer 3: PIP – add 1 cup capsicum cut to stamp-size, 2tsp each caramelized (onion, tomato, cashew paste, ginger-garlic paste), 1/2tsp each (salt, Kashmiri chilli powder, garam masala powder)

Cook on high for 3 whistles or 4 minutes. Release pressure. Mix everything with 1tbsp almond slivers.

Thursday: Kadhai Mixed Vegetable Egg Masala

In a 2L Pressure Baker, layer as below:
Layer 1: 2tbsp oil
Layer 2: 1 cup French-cut beans
Layer 3: 1/2 cup sliced carrot
Layer 4: 1/2 cup each (capsicum cut to stamp-size, cauliflower florets cut to bite size) mixed with 2tbsp each caramelized (onion, tomato), 1tsp each (ginger-garlic paste, Kashmiri chilli powder), 1/2tsp each (salt, garam masala powder)
Layer 5: 2 well-washed eggs

Cook on high for 2 whistles or 4 minutes. Release pressure. Let eggs cool. Peel and halve. Mix everything with 1/4 cup milk.

Friday: Kadhai Murgh

In a 2L Pressure Baker, layer as below:
Layer 1: 2tbsp oil
Layer 2: 1 cup onion petals cut to stamp-size
Layer 3: 250g chopped chicken mixed with 1tsp ginger-garlic paste, 1/2tsp each (salt, Kashmiri chilli powder, garam masala powder)

Cook on high for 5 whistles or 6 minutes. Release pressure. Mix in 1/2 cup chopped capsicum.

Saturday: Kadhai Gosht

In a 2L Pressure Baker, layer as below:
Layer 1: 2tbsp oil
Layer 2: 250g chopped boneless tender mutton mixed with 1/4tsp each (salt, turmeric powder)
Layer 3: PIP – add 1tbsp each caramelized (onion, tomato), 1tsp ginger-garlic paste, 1/2tsp each (salt, Kashmiri chilli powder, garam masala powder)

Cook on high for 8 minutes. Let pressure settle. Mix in 1/2 cup chopped capsicum, 1/4 cup whisked yogurt.

Sunday: Kadhai Jhinga

In a 2L Pressure Baker, layer as below:
Layer 1: 2tbsp oil
Layer 2: 250g prawns mixed with 1/4tsp each (salt, turmeric powder)
Layer 3: PIP – add 1/2 cup capsicum cut to bite size, 1tbsp each caramelized (onion, tomato), 1tsp ginger-garlic paste, 1/2tsp each (Kashmiri chilli powder, garam masala powder), 1/4tsp salt

Cook on high for 3 whistles or 4 minutes. Release pressure. Mix everything.

KERALA AVIYAL (MIXED VEGETABLES WITH SOUR COCONUT SAUCE)

Base: Mixed Vegetables, Other Edibles, Coconut Paste, Souring Agent
Flavouring: Coconut Oil, Curry Leaves, Curry Paste; tadka is rarely used
Additives: Yogurt, Buttermilk, Water, Stock, Coconut Milk or any edible liquid

Monday: Classic Aviyal

Prep.: Blend 1/2 cup chopped coconut, 4 green chillies, each (salt, coconut oil, cumin), 1/4 cup water to a thick paste.

In a 2L Pressure Baker, layer as below:
Layer 1: 1/4 cup water
Layer 2: 1/2 cup each (beans cut into fingers, raw banana and carrot cut into thin fingers, white pumpkin cut into thick fingers)
Layer 3: Coconut paste (see prep.)

Cook on high for 3 whistles or 5 minutes. Release pressure. Mix in 1/4 cup whisked yogurt, 5 crushed curry leaves. Mix in 1/4 cup water/ buttermilk to convert it into Aviyal Kuzhambu.

Tuesday: Vegan Aviyal/Puli Aviyal

Prep.: Blend 1/2 cup chopped coconut, 2tsp tamarind paste, 4 green chillies, 1tsp each (salt, coconut oil, cumin), 1/4 cup water to a thick paste.

In a 2L Pressure Baker, layer as below:
Layer 1: 1/4 cup water
Layer 2: 1/2 cup each (beans cut into fingers, raw banana and carrot cut into thin fingers, white pumpkin cut into thick fingers)
Layer 3: Coconut paste (see prep.)

Cook on high for 3 whistles or 5 minutes. Release pressure. Mix in 5 crushed curry leaves.

Wednesday: Thengapaal Aviyal (Coconut Milk Aviyal)

Prep.: Blend 1/4 cup raw mango, 2tbsp roasted chana dal, 3 green chillies, 1tsp each (cumin, salt, coconut oil) to a thick paste.

In a 2L Pressure Baker, layer as below:
Layer 1: 1/4 cup water
Layer 2: 1/2 cup each (beans cut into fingers, raw banana and carrot cut into thin fingers, white pumpkin cut into thick fingers)
Layer 3: Spice paste (see prep.)

Cook on high for 3 whistles or 5 minutes. Release pressure. Mix in 5 crushed curry leaves, 1/4 cup coconut milk.

Thursday: Chettinad Kalla Veetu Aviyal

Prep.: Blend 1/4 cup chopped coconut, 2tbsp each caramelized (onion, tomato), 5 each (cashews, dry red chillies), 1 garlic clove, 1tsp each (salt, coconut oil, fennel), 1/4tsp each (garam masala powder, turmeric), 1/8 cup water to a thick paste.

In a 2L Pressure Baker, layer as below:
Layer 1: 1/4 cup water
Layer 2: 1 cup potato chopped into small cubes
Layer 3: 1 cup brinjal cut to bite size
Layer 4: Coconut paste (see prep.)

Cook on high for 3 whistles or 5 minutes. Release pressure. Mix everything with 1/2 cup water.

Friday: Mutta Aviyal (Egg Aviyal)

Prep.: Blend 1/2 cup chopped coconut, 1 garlic clove, 4 green chillies, 1tsp each (salt, cumin, coconut oil), 1/4tsp turmeric, 1/4 cup water to a thick paste.

In a 2L Pressure Baker, layer as below:
Layer 1: 1/4 cup water
Layer 2: 1/2 cup each (beans cut into fingers, raw banana and carrot cut into thin fingers, white pumpkin cut into thick fingers)
Layer 3: Coconut paste (see prep.)
Layer 4: 2 well-washed eggs

Cook on high for 3 whistles or 5 minutes. Release pressure. Remove eggs, let cool completely and peel. Mix everything with 5 crushed curry leaves.

Saturday: Paleo Aviyal

Prep.: Blend 1/2 cup chopped coconut, 5 overnight soaked and drained almonds, 4 green chillies, 1tsp each (salt, cumin), 2tbsp cold-pressed coconut oil, 1/4 cup water to a thick paste.

In a 2L Pressure Baker, layer as below:
Layer 1: 1/4 cup water, 1tbsp cold-pressed coconut oil
Layer 2: 1/2 cup each (carrots, squash and snake gourd chopped into thin fingers, white pumpkin chopped into thick fingers)
Layer 3: Coconut paste (see prep.)
Layer 4: 2 well-washed eggs

Cook on high for 3 whistles or 5 minutes. Release pressure. Remove eggs, let cool completely and peel and cut in half. Mix everything with 5 crushed curry leaves.

Sunday: Nethili Aviyal (Fish Aviyal)

Prep.: Mix 250g anchovies with 1/4tsp turmeric powder, 1/2tsp salt. Wash and drain. Blend 1/2 cup chopped coconut, 4 dry red chillies, 3 shallots, 1 garlic clove, 1tsp each (salt, coconut oil), 1/4 cup water to a thick paste.

In a 2L Pressure Baker, layer as below:
Layer 1: 2tbsp coconut oil
Layer 2: Anchovies

Layer 3: Coconut paste (see prep.) in a shallow plate
Cook on high for 1 whistle or 4 minutes. Release pressure. Remove plate
and mix coconut paste with 1/2 cup water. Pour over fish and serve.

Tip

If coconut paste is not thick, use PIP.

NORTH INDIAN BHARTA (SPICED MASH)

Base: Non-watery Vegetables, Meat, Fish, Eggs, Seafood, Sprouts, Lentils
Flavouring: Oil, Bottled Tadka
Additives: Onion, Chillies, Lemon Juice

Monday: Classic Baingan Bharta

In a 2L Pressure Baker, layer as below:
Layer 1: 2tbsp oil
Layer 2: 250g chopped brinjal arranged in a single layer
Layer 3: 2 chopped green chillies, 1tsp ginger-garlic paste, 1/2tsp each
(salt, garam masala powder)

Cook on high for 4 whistles or 5 minutes. Release pressure. Mash. Mix
in 1/4 cup finely chopped onion, 1tsp lemon juice.

Tuesday: Tomato Paneer Bharta

Mix 1 cup chopped paneer, 1tsp ginger-garlic paste, 1/2tsp each (salt,
chilli powder, garam masala powder)

In a 2L Pressure Baker, layer as below:
Layer 1: 2tbsp butter
Layer 2: 1 cup chopped tomato
Layer 3: PIP – spiced paneer

Cook on high for 4 whistles or 5 minutes. Release pressure. Mash
everything. Mix in 1/4 cup finely chopped onion, 2tbsp chopped cilantro.

Wednesday: Matar Bharta

In a 2L Pressure Baker, layer as below:
Layer 1: 1tbsp oil, 1/4 cup water
Layer 2: 2 cups fresh green peas, 1 chopped green chilli
Layer 3: 1/2tsp each (salt, garam masala powder) a pinch of asafoetida

Cook on high for 2 whistles or 4 minutes. Release pressure. Mash everything. Mix in 1/2tsp lemon juice.

Thursday: Masoor Dal Bharta

Soak 1/2 cup masoor dal for 2 hours. Drain.

In a 2L Pressure Baker, layer as below:
Layer 1: 2tbsp ghee, 1/4 cup water
Layer 2: Masoor dal
Layer 3: 2 chopped green chillies, 1tsp ginger-garlic paste, 1/2tsp each (salt, garam masala powder)

Cook on high for 4 whistles or 5 minutes. Let pressure settle. Mash. Mix in 1/4 cup finely chopped onion, 1tsp lemon juice.

Friday: Bengali Aloo Dim Bharta

In a 2L Pressure Baker, layer as below:
Layer 1: 1tbsp oil, 1/4 cup water
Layer 2: 2 cups potato chopped small
Layer 3: 2 well-washed eggs

Cook on high for 4 whistles or 5 minutes. Let pressure settle. Peel eggs. Mash everything. Mix in 1/4 cup finely chopped onion, 2 finely chopped green chillies, 1/2tsp salt, 1tsp mustard oil.

Saturday: Kele ka Bharta

In a 2L Pressure Baker, layer as below:
Layer 1: 1tbsp oil, 1/4 cup water
Layer 2: 2 cups raw banana chopped small
Layer 3: 1tsp grated ginger, 1/2tsp each (salt, chilli powder, amchur), a pinch of asafoetida

Cook on high for 2 whistles or 4 minutes. Let pressure settle. Mash everything. Mix in 1 finely chopped green chilli.

Sunday: Tripuri Chicken Bharta

In a 2L Pressure Baker, layer as below:
Layer 1: 1tbsp oil
Layer 2: 250g boneless chicken mixed with 1/2tsp salt, 1tbsp ginger-garlic paste, 3 chopped green chillies

Cook on high for 5 whistles or 6 minutes. Let pressure settle. Flake chicken. Mix in 1/2 cup sliced onion, 1/2tsp pepper.

KERALA ISHTU (COCONUT MILK STEW)

Base: Coconut Milk, Vegetables, Poultry, Meat, Fish, Seafood, Eggs
Flavouring: Pepper, Ginger, Curry Leaves, Coconut Oil
Additives: Fried Onion

Monday: Classic Ishtu

In a 2L Pressure Baker, layer as below:
Layer 1: 1tbsp oil, 2tsp water
Layer 2: 1 cup thinly sliced onion, 2 slit green chillies, 1tsp grated ginger
Layer 3: 2 cups mixed vegetables, 1/2tsp salt

Cook on high for 2 whistles or 4 minutes. Release pressure. Mash coarsely. Mix in 1/2 cup each (coconut milk, water), 5 crushed curry leaves, 1tsp coconut oil, 1/2tsp pepper.

Tuesday: Mix Veg Ishtu

In a 2L Pressure Baker, layer as below:
Layer 1: 1/4 cup thin coconut milk
Layer 2: 2 cups mixed vegetables, 2 slit green chillies, 1tsp grated ginger

Cook on high for 2 whistles or 4 minutes. Release pressure. Mash coarsely. Mix in 1/2 cup each (coconut milk, water), 5 crushed curry leaves, 1tsp coconut oil, 1/2tsp each (pepper, salt).

Wednesday: Chicken Ishtu

In a 2L Pressure Baker, layer as below:
Layer 1: 1tbsp oil
Layer 2: 2 cups chicken chopped small, 3 slit green chillies
Layer 3: 1/2 cup each chopped (potato, carrot [big]) mixed with 1tsp ginger-garlic paste, 1/2tsp garam masala powder, 1tbsp cashew powder

Cook on high for 5 whistles or 6 minutes. Release pressure. Mash potato and carrot. Mix in 1/2 cup each (coconut milk, water), 5 crushed curry leaves, 1tsp coconut oil, 1/2tsp each (pepper, salt).

Thursday: Mutton Ishtu

In a 2L Pressure Baker, layer as below:
Layer 1: 1tbsp ghee
Layer 2: 1/2 cup each chopped (shallots, tomato) 3 slit green chillies
Layer 3: 2 cups tender mutton chopped small mixed with 1tsp ginger-garlic paste, 1/2tsp each (garam masala powder, salt)
Layer 4: 1/2 cup chopped potato

Cook on high for 7 whistles or 8 minutes. Let pressure settle. Mash potato. Mix in 1/2 cup each (coconut milk, water), 5 crushed curry leaves, 1tsp coconut oil, 1/2tsp pepper.

Friday: Mutta Ishtu (Egg Stew)

In a 2L Pressure Baker, layer as below:
Layer 1: 1 tbsp oil
Layer 2: 1/2 cup each chopped (shallots, tomato), 3 slit green chillies
Layer 3: 4 well-washed eggs

Cook on high for 3 whistles or 5 minutes. Let pressure settle. Peel and halve eggs. Remove 2 yolks. Mash yolks with 1/2 cup each (coconut milk, water), 5 crushed curry leaves, 1 tsp coconut oil, 1/2 tsp pepper. Mix everything.

Saturday: Kappa Ishtu (Tapioca Stew)

In a 2L Pressure Baker, layer as below:
Layer 1: 1/4 cup thin coconut milk
Layer 2: 2 cups tapioca chopped small, 2 slit green chillies, 1 tsp grated ginger

Cook on high for 4 whistles or 5 minutes. Let pressure settle. Mash coarsely. Mix in 1/2 each (coconut milk, water), 5 crushed curry leaves, 1 tsp coconut oil, 1/2 tsp each (pepper, salt).

Sunday: Chemmeen Ishtu (Prawn Stew)

In a 2L Pressure Baker, layer as below:
Layer 1: 1 tbsp oil
Layer 2: 1 cup thinly sliced onion, 2 slit green chillies, 1 tsp grated ginger
Layer 3: 2 cups prawns mixed with 1/2 tsp each (salt, garam masala powder, ginger-garlic paste)

Cook on high for 3 whistles or 4 minutes. Release pressure. Mix in 1/2 cup each (coconut milk, water), 5 crushed curry leaves, 1 tsp coconut oil, 1/2 tsp pepper.

Tip

Can keep coconut milk in an inner vessel if you want a cooked taste.

NORTH INDIAN KADHI (GRAM FLOUR SOUR STEW)

Base: Gram Flour
Flavouring: Chillies, Turmeric, Fenugreek, Asafoetida, Bottled Tadka (p. 26)
Additives: Pakodi, Wadiyan, Kofta, Spinach, Boondi, Vegetables, Sprouts

Monday: Classic Kadhi

Prep.: Mix 2tbsp roasted gram flour with 1 cup buttermilk, 1/2tsp each (salt, chilli powder), 1/4tsp turmeric powder, a pinch of fenugreek powder.

In a 2L Pressure Baker, add 1/2 cup thin buttermilk. Place the vessel with gram flour mix.

Cook on high for 7 minutes. Let pressure settle. Mix everything with 1tbsp bottled tadka, 1/2 cup ready-made pakodi/vada/boondi. Let steep for 10 minutes.

Tuesday: Sindhi Kadhi

Prep.: Mix 2tbsp roasted gram flour with 1 cup water, 1/2tsp each (salt, grated ginger), 1/4tsp turmeric powder.

In a 2L Pressure Baker, layer as below:
Layer 1: 2tbsp oil
Layer 2: 1 cup chopped tomato, 2 slit green chillies
Layer 3: 1 cup chopped mixed vegetables
Layer 4: PIP – gram flour mix (see prep.)

Cook on high for 5 minutes. Release pressure. Remove PIP. Mix everything with 1tbsp bottled tadka. Let steep for 10 minutes.

Wednesday: Dal Kadhi

Prep.: Soak 1/2 cup moong/masoor dal for 2 hours. Drain. Mix 1 cup buttermilk, 1/2tsp each (salt, chilli powder), 1/4tsp turmeric powder, a pinch of fenugreek powder.

In a 2L Pressure Baker, layer as below:
Layer 1: 1tbsp oil, 1/4 cup buttermilk
Layer 2: Dal
Layer 3: PIP – buttermilk mix (see prep.)

Cook on high for 6 minutes. Let pressure settle. Remove PIP. Mash dal. Mix everything with 1tbsp bottled tadka, 1/4 cup ready-made boondi. Let steep for 10 minutes.

Thursday: Gatte ki Kadhi

Prep.: Take 1/2 cup roasted gram flour, 1/2tsp each (chilli powder, salt, grated ginger). Add 1tbsp yogurt. Knead into a stiff dough. Pinch off small bits. Mix 2tbsp roasted gram flour with 1 cup buttermilk, 1/2tsp each (salt, chilli powder), 1/4tsp turmeric powder, a pinch of fenugreek powder, 1/2 cup gram flour dumplings.

In a 2L Pressure Baker, layer as below:
Layer 1: 1tbsp oil
Layer 2: 1/2 cup thin buttermilk
Layer 3: PIP – gram flour mix (see prep.)

Cook on high for 7 minutes. Let pressure settle. Remove PIP. Mix everything with 1tbsp bottled tadka. Let steep for 10 minutes.

Friday: Vrat ki Kadhi

Prep.: Mix 2tbsp water chestnut (singhara)/buckwheat (kuttu) flour with 1 cup buttermilk, 1/2tsp each (salt, chilli powder), 1/4tsp turmeric powder, a pinch of fenugreek powder.

In a 2L Pressure Baker, add 1/2 cup thin buttermilk. Place the vessel with the flour mix.

Cook on high for 7 minutes. Let pressure settle. Mix everything with 1tbsp bottled tadka, 1/2 cup ready-made pakodi/vada/boondi. Let steep for 10 minutes.

Saturday: Kofta Kadhi

Prep.: Soak 1/2 cup moong/masoor dal for 2 hours. Drain. Blend to a coarse paste with 2 green chillies, 1/2tsp salt. Shape into marble-sized balls. Mix 2tbsp roasted gram flour, 2 cups buttermilk, 1/2tsp each (salt, chilli powder), 1/4tsp turmeric powder, a pinch of fenugreek powder, dal balls.

In a 2L Pressure Baker, layer as below:
Layer 1: 1tbsp oil, 1/2 cup buttermilk
Layer 2: PIP – buttermilk mix (see prep.)

Cook on high for 7 minutes. Let pressure settle. Mix everything with 1tbsp bottled tadka. Let steep for 10 minutes.

Sunday: Palak Kadhi

Prep.: Mix 2tbsp roasted gram flour with 1 cup buttermilk, 1/2tsp salt, 1/4tsp turmeric powder, a pinch of fenugreek powder.

In a 2L Pressure Baker, layer as below:
Layer 1: 1tbsp oil, 1/4 cup thin buttermilk
Layer 2: 2 cups chopped spinach, 2 slit green chillies
Layer 3: PIP – gram flour mix (see prep.)

Cook on high for 5 minutes. Release pressure. Mix everything with 1tbsp bottled tadka. Let steep for 10 minutes.

Common tadka:

Mustard seeds, dry red chilli, asafoetida, cumin seeds, fenugreek in oil.

Tips

1. For Gujarati kadhi, mix in 1/2tsp sugar.
2. Can mix in 1/4 cup whisked yogurt on opening.

TAMIL KOOTU (COCONUT–LENTIL–VEGETABLE STEW)

Base: Vegetables, Sprouts, Greens, Coconut Paste, Dal
Flavouring: Coconut Oil, Ghee, Cumin, Bottled Tadka (p. 26)
Additives: Milk, Yogurt, Water, Stock, Coconut Milk

Monday: Classic Kootu

Prep.: Blend 1/4 cup chopped coconut, 1tsp each (cumin, salt, oil), 1 green chilli, 2tbsp water to a thick paste.

In a 2L Pressure Baker, layer as below:
Layer 1: 1/4 cup water
Layer 2: 1/2 cup each chopped (carrot, beans, potato)
Layer 3: Coconut spice paste (see prep.), 1/4 cup cooked dal

Cook on high for 3 whistles or 5 minutes. Release pressure. Mix in 1/4 cup water, 1tsp bottled tadka.

Tuesday: Appala Kootu

Prep.: Soak 1/4 cup moong dal in water for 2 hours. Drain. Blend 1/4 cup chopped coconut, 1tsp each (cumin, salt, oil), 1 green chilli, 2tbsp water to a thick paste.

In a 2L Pressure Baker, layer as below:
Layer 1: 1/4 cup water
Layer 2: Moong dal
Layer 3: 1/4 cup torn papad/kootu vadaam (sun-dried lentil paste)
Layer 4: Coconut spice paste (see prep.)

Cook on high for 3 whistles or 5 minutes. Let pressure settle. Mash dal. Mix in 1/4 cup water, 1tsp bottled tadka.

Wednesday: Mixed Sprouts Kootu

Prep.: Soak 1/4 cup chana/tuvar dal in water overnight. Drain. Blend 1/4 cup chopped coconut, 1tsp each (cumin, salt, oil), 1 green chilli, 2tbsp water to a thick paste.

In a 2L Pressure Baker, layer as below:
Layer 1: 1/4 cup water
Layer 2: Dal
Layer 3: 1/2 cup sprouts
Layer 4: Coconut spice paste (see prep.)

Cook on high for 4 whistles or 6 minutes. Let pressure settle. Mix in 1/4 cup water, 1tsp bottled tadka.

Thursday: Thenga Pal Kootu

Prep.: Blend 1/4 cup roasted gram, 1tsp each (cumin, salt, oil), 1 green chilli, 1/4 cup water, a pinch each (turmeric powder, asafoetida) to a thick paste.

In a 2L Pressure Baker, layer as below:
Layer 1: 1/4 cup water
Layer 2: 2 cups chopped vegetables
Layer 3: Spice paste (see prep.), 1/4 cup cooked dal

Cook on high for 3 whistles or 5 minutes. Release pressure. Mix in 1/4 cup coconut milk, 1tsp bottled tadka.

Friday: Chettinad Kootu

In a 2L Pressure Baker, layer as below:
Layer 1: 2tbsp ghee
Layer 2: 1/2 cup chopped shallots, 1 chopped green chilli

Layer 3: 2 cups chopped snake gourd
Layer 4: 3/4 cup cooked dal, 1 tsp sambar powder, a pinch each (turmeric powder, asafoetida)

Cook on high for 3 whistles or 5 minutes. Release pressure. Mix in 1/4 cup water, 1 tsp bottled tadka.

Saturday: Podi Potta Thayir Kootu

Prep.: Blend 1/4 cup coconut, 2 tbsp spiced lentil powder, 1 tsp each (cumin, salt, oil), 1 green chilli, 2 tbsp water to a thick paste.

In a 2L Pressure Baker, layer as below:
Layer 1: 1/4 cup water
Layer 2: 1/2 cup each chopped (cluster beans, French beans, long beans, broad beans)
Layer 3: Coconut spice paste (see prep.)

Cook on high for 3 whistles or 5 minutes. Release pressure. Mix in 1/4 cup yogurt, 1 tsp bottled tadka.

Sunday: Mupparuppu Puli Kootu

Prep.: Soak 1 tbsp each dal (masoor, moong, tuvar, chana) overnight. Drain. Blend 1/4 cup coconut, 1/2 tsp each (cumin, salt, oil), 1 dry red chilli, 2 tbsp water, 1 tsp tamarind paste to a thick paste.

In a 2L Pressure Baker, layer as below:
Layer 1: 1/4 cup water
Layer 2: Dal
Layer 3: 1/2 cup each chopped (raw banana, yam)
Layer 4: Coconut spice paste (see prep.)

Cook on high for 4 whistles or 6 minutes. Let pressure settle. Mix in 1/4 cup water, 1 tsp bottled tadka.

Tip

If spice paste is not thick, use PIP.

MUGHLAI KORMA (NUT- AND DAIRY-BASED STEW)

Base: Vegetables, Egg, Meat, Fish, Seafood, Other Edibles, Nut Paste
Flavouring: Garam Masala Powder, Ginger-garlic Paste (p. 28), Bottled Tadka (p. 26)
Additives: Caramelized Onion/Tomato (p. 29) Milk, Cream, Yogurt, Water, Stock (p. 53-54), Coconut Milk, Other Plant Milk or any edible liquid

Monday: Classic Mughlai Korma

Prep.: Blend 1/4 cup soaked almonds, 1tsp each (ginger-garlic paste, salt), 1/2tsp garam masala powder, 1 green chilli, 2tbsp water to a thick paste.

In a 2L Pressure Baker, layer as below:
Layer 1: 1/4 cup water
Layer 2: 1/2 cup each chopped (carrot, beans, potato)
Layer 3: Nut paste (see prep.), 5 crushed mint leaves, PIP – 1/2 cup each (green peas, cubed paneer)

Cook on high for 3 whistles or 5 minutes. Release pressure. Mix in 1/2 cup whisked yogurt.

Tuesday: Navratan Korma

Prep.: Soak 1/2tbsp each seeds (poppy [khus khus], melon). Drain. Blend with 1tsp each (ginger-garlic paste, salt), 1/2tsp garam masala powder, 1 green chilli, 2tbsp water to a thick paste.

In a 2L Pressure Baker, layer as below:
Layer 1: 1/4 cup water
Layer 2: 1 cup chopped mixed vegetables (carrot, beans, potato)
Layer 3: PIP – spice paste (see prep.), 1/4 cup each (capsicum, peas, pineapple, cauliflower, raisins)

Cook on high for 3 whistles or 5 minutes. Release pressure. Mix in 1/4 cup cream.

Wednesday: HSB Kuruma (Vegan)

See p. 38 for recipe.

See p. 38 for recipe.

Thursday: Dal Korma (Vegan/Jain)

Prep.: Soak 1/2 cup dal (moong/masoor/chana/tuvar) for 1 hour. Blend 1/4 cup cashew, 1tsp each (ginger, fennel, salt), 1/2tsp garam masala powder, 1 green chilli, a pinch of turmeric powder, 2tbsp water to a thick paste.

In a 2L Pressure Baker, layer as below:
Layer 1: 1/4 cup water, 1tbsp ghee
Layer 2: Dal
Layer 3: Spice paste (see prep.)

Cook on high for 4 whistles or 6 minutes. Let pressure settle. Mix in 1/2 cup coconut milk.

Friday: Chicken Korma

Prep.: Blend 1/4 cup cashew, 1tsp each (ginger-garlic paste, salt), 1/2tsp garam masala powder, 1 green chilli, 1tbsp each caramelized (onion, tomato) to a thick paste.

In a 2L Pressure Baker, layer as below:
Layer 1: 2tbsp oil
Layer 2: 250g chicken mixed with 1/2tsp salt, a pinch of turmeric powder
Layer 3: Spice paste (see prep.)

Cook on high for 5 whistles or 6 minutes. Release pressure. Mix everything with 1/4 cup stock.

Saturday: Egg Korma (Paleo)

Prep.: Blend 1/4 cup cashew, 1tsp each (ginger-garlic paste, salt, pepper), 1/2tsp garam masala powder, 1 green chilli to a thick paste.

In a 2L Pressure Baker, layer as below:
Layer 1: 2tbsp cold-pressed coconut oil
Layer 2: 1 cup each chopped (onion, deseeded tomato) arranged in a bull's-eye method
Layer 3: Place 2 well-washed eggs
Layer 4: PIP – spice paste (see prep.)

Cook on high for 4 whistles or 5 minutes. Let pressure settle. Remove eggs, peel and halve. Mash gravy. Mix everything with 1/4 cup water.

Sunday: Fish Korma (Paleo)

Prep.: Mix 250g chopped fish with 1/2tsp salt, 1tsp ginger-garlic paste, a pinch of turmeric powder, 1/4tsp salt. Blend 1/4 cup soaked almonds, 1/2tsp each (salt, garam masala powder), 1 green chilli, 2tbsp water to a thick paste.

In a 2L Pressure Baker, layer as below:
Layer 1: 3tbsp ghee
Layer 2: Fish, 1/4 cup potato chopped small
Layer 3: PIP – spice paste

Cook on high for 2 whistles or 5 minutes. Release pressure. Remove PIP and mix spice paste with 1/2 cup coconut milk. Pour over fish and serve.

TAMIL MILAGU PERATTAL (PEPPER STIR-FRY)

Base: Vegetables, Egg, Meat, Fish, Seafood, Other Edibles, Pepper
Flavouring: Bottled Tadka (p. 26), Spices, Ginger-garlic Paste (p. 28)
Additives: Spiced Lentil Powder (p. 31), Caramelized Onion/Tomato (p. 29)

Monday: Classic Milagu Perattal

Prep.: Blend 1tbsp roasted peppercorns, 1tsp roasted cumin, 2 roasted dry red chillies, 3 dry curry leaves to a coarse powder.

In a 2L Pressure Baker, layer as below:
Layer 1: 2tbsp water, 1tbsp oil
Layer 2: 2 cups chopped starchy vegetables (potato/raw banana/colocasia/yam/sweet corn)
Layer 3: 1tsp ginger-garlic paste, 1/2tsp salt

Cook on high for 2 whistles or 5 minutes. Let pressure settle. Mix in blended powder.

Tuesday: Delicate Vegetables Milagu Perattal

In a 2L Pressure Baker, layer as below:
Layer 1: 1/4 cup water
Layer 2: PIP – 250g delicate vegetables chopped (cauliflower/capsicum/green peas/baby corn) mixed with 1tbsp crushed pepper, 1/2tsp salt, 1tsp ginger-garlic paste

Cook on high for 2 whistles or 5 minutes. Release pressure. Mix in 1tbsp bottled tadka.

Wednesday: Egg Milagu Perattal

Prep.: Blend 1tbsp roasted peppercorns, 1tsp roasted cumin, 2 roasted dry red chillies, 3 dry curry leaves to a coarse powder.

In a 2L Pressure Baker, layer as below:
Layer 1: 2tbsp oil
Layer 2: 1 cup chopped onion, 2 chopped green chillies
Layer 3: 1tsp ginger-garlic paste, 1/2tsp salt, 4 well-washed eggs

Cook on high for 2 whistles or 4 minutes. Let pressure settle. Remove eggs. Let cool. Peel and quarter. Mix everything with blended powder.

Thursday: Chettinad Milagu Perattal

Prep.: Blend 1tbsp roasted peppercorns, 1tsp each roasted (cumin, fennel), 1 roasted dry red chilli, 3 dry curry leaves to a coarse powder.

In a 2L Pressure Baker, layer as below:
Layer 1: 2tbsp oil
Layer 2: 2 cups chopped non-watery vegetables (carrots, French beans, cluster beans, cabbage, beetroot, bitter gourd, snake gourd [chachinda], ivy gourd [kundru/parwal])
Layer 3: 1tsp ginger-garlic paste, 1/2tsp salt

Cook on high for 2 whistles or 5 minutes. Let pressure settle. Mix in blended powder.

Friday: Kongunadu Chicken Milagu Perattal

Prep.: Blend 1tbsp each (roasted peppercorns, grated copra), 1tsp each (roasted cumin, fennel), 1 roasted dry red chilli, 3 dry curry leaves to a coarse powder.

In a 2L Pressure Baker, layer as below:
Layer 1: 2tbsp oil
Layer 2: 250g chopped chicken mixed with 1/4tsp each (salt, turmeric powder), 1tsp ginger-garlic paste, 1tbsp caramelized onion

Cook on high for 5 whistles or 6 minutes. Let pressure settle. Mix in blended powder.

Saturday: Nandu Milagu Perattal

Prep.: Blend 1tbsp roasted peppercorns, 1tsp each roasted seeds (cumin, fennel), 1 roasted dry red chilli, 3 dry curry leaves, 1/2tsp salt to a coarse powder.

In a 2L Pressure Baker, layer as below:
Layer 1: 2tbsp oil
Layer 2: 250g cleaned crab mixed with 1/4tsp each (salt, turmeric powder), 1tsp ginger-garlic paste, 1tbsp caramelized onion

Cook on high for 3 whistles or 5 minutes. Let pressure settle. Mix in blended powder.

Sunday: Era Milagu Perattal

Prep.: Blend 1tbsp roasted peppercorns, 1tsp each roasted seeds (cumin, fennel, khus khus), 1 roasted dry red chilli, 3 dry curry leaves to a coarse powder.

In a 2L Pressure Baker, layer as below:
Layer 1: 2tbsp oil
Layer 2: 250g cleaned prawns mixed with 1/4tsp each (salt, turmeric powder), 1tsp ginger-garlic paste, 1tbsp caramelized (onion, tomato)

Cook on high for 3 whistles or 5 minutes. Let pressure settle. Mix in blended powder.

Common tadka:

Mustard seeds, dry red chillies, curry leaves.

Tip

Replace blended spice powder with spiced lentil powder for podi kari.

PALAKKAD MOLAGOOTAL
(COCONUT–LENTIL–VEGETABLE STEW)

Base: Mixed Vegetables, Spinach, Sprouts, Coconut, Dal
Flavouring: Coconut Oil, Bottled Tadka (p. 26)
Additives: Roasted Lentil Powder

Monday: Classic Molagootal

Prep.: Blend 1/4 cup coconut, 1 dry red chilli, 1/2tsp each (salt, cumin), a pinch of turmeric powder, 1/4 cup water to a paste.

In a 2L Pressure Baker, layer as below:
Layer 1: 1/4 cup water
Layer 2: 2 cups mixed vegetables
Layer 3: Coconut paste (see prep.), 1/2 cup cooked tuvar dal

Cook on high for 3 whistles or 5 minutes. Release pressure. Mix everything with 1/4 cup water, 1tsp bottled tadka.

Tuesday: Keerai Molagootal

Prep.: Blend 1/4 cup coconut, 1 dry red chilli, 1/2tsp each (salt, cumin), 1tbsp each (roasted urad dal, water), a pinch of turmeric powder to a paste.

In a 2L Pressure Baker, layer as below:
Layer 1: 1/4 cup water
Layer 2: 4 cups chopped spinach (any variety)
Layer 3: Spice paste (see prep.), 1/4 cup cooked tuvar dal

Cook on high for 2 whistles or 5 minutes. Release pressure. Mash everything with 1/4 cup water, 1tbsp bottled tadka.

Wednesday: Vazhakka Molagootal

Prep.: Soak 1/4 cup moong dal for 3 hours. Drain. Blend 1/4 cup coconut, 1 dry red chilli, 1tbsp spiced lentil powder, 1/2tsp each (salt, cumin), a pinch of turmeric powder to a paste.

In a 2L Pressure Baker, layer as below:
Layer 1: 1/4 cup water
Layer 2: Dal
Layer 3: 2 cups chopped raw banana
Layer 4: Spice paste (see prep.)

Cook on high for 3 whistles or 5 minutes. Let pressure settle. Mash dal. Mix everything with 1/4 cup water, bottled tadka.

Thursday: Sprouts Molagootal

Prep.: Blend 1/4 cup spiced coconut powder (thengai molagapodi), 1 dry red chilli, 1/2tsp each (salt, cumin), a pinch of turmeric powder, 1tsp coconut oil, 2tbsp water to a paste.

In a 2L Pressure Baker, layer as below:
Layer 1: 1/4 cup water
Layer 2: 2 cups mixed sprouts
Layer 3: Spiced coconut paste (see prep.), 1/4 cup cooked tuvar dal

Cook on high for 3 whistles or 5 minutes. Release pressure. Mix in 1/4 cup water, 1tsp bottled tadka.

Friday: Elavan Molagootal

Prep.: Blend 1/4 cup coconut, 1tbsp pepper, 1/2tsp each (salt, cumin), a pinch of turmeric powder, 1tsp coconut oil, 2tbsp water to a paste.

In a 2L Pressure Baker, layer as below:
Layer 1: 1/4 cup water
Layer 2: 2 cups chopped white pumpkin
Layer 3: Spice paste (see prep.), 1/4 cup cooked tuvar dal

Cook on high for 2 whistles or 5 minutes. Release pressure. Mix in 1/4 cup water, 1tsp bottled tadka.

Saturday: Mathan Molagootal

Prep.: Blend 1/4 cup chammanthi podi (spiced coconut powder), 1/4tsp each (salt, cumin), a pinch of turmeric powder, 1tsp coconut oil, 2tbsp water to a paste.

In a 2L Pressure Baker, layer as below:
Layer 1: 1/4 cup water
Layer 2: 2 cups chopped squash
Layer 3: Spice paste (see prep.), 1/4 cup cooked tuvar dal

Cook on high for 2 whistles or 5 minutes. Release pressure. Mix in 1/4 cup water, 1tsp bottled tadka.

Sunday: Mulakushyam

Prep.: Blend 1 dry red chilli, 1tsp pepper, 1/2tsp each (salt, cumin), a pinch of turmeric powder, 1tsp each (pepper, coconut oil), 1tbsp water to a paste.

In a 2L Pressure Baker, layer as below:
Layer 1: 1/4 cup water
Layer 2: 2 cups mixed vegetables
Layer 3: Spice paste (see prep.) 1/2 cup cooked tuvar dal

Cook on high for 3 whistles or 5 minutes. Release pressure. Mix everything with 1tsp bottled tadka.

Common tadka:

Mustard seeds, dry red chillies, split urad dal, asafoetida, curry leaves in coconut oil.

Tip

If spice paste is not thick, use PIP.

TAMIL MOREKUZHAMBU (SOUTH INDIAN KADHI/YOGURT STEW)

Base: Yogurt, Soaked Lentils, Coconut, Vegetables, Vegetable Substitutes
Flavouring: Chillies, Turmeric, Asafoetida, Bottled Tadka (p. 26)
Additives: Buttermilk, Stock (p. 53-54), Roasted Gram Flour, Rice/Lentil Paste

Monday: Classic Morekuzhambu

Prep.: Blend 1/2 cup chopped coconut, 4 green chillies, 1tsp each soaked (tuvar dal, rice [optional], coriander seeds, cumin), 1/2tsp salt, 1/4tsp turmeric powder, 1/4 cup water to a thick paste.

In a 2L Pressure Baker, layer as below:
Layer 1: 1/4 cup thin buttermilk

Layer 2: 1 cup each chopped (chow chow, white pumpkin, ladyfinger, colocasia, apple, pineapple)
Layer 3: Coconut spice paste (see prep.)

Cook on high for 3 whistles or 5 minutes. Release pressure. Mix in 1/2 cup whisked yogurt, 1 tsp bottled tadka.

Tuesday: Instant Morekuzhambu

Prep.: Mix 1 tbsp roasted gram flour, 1 tsp each (rice flour [optional], sambar powder, chopped [ginger, chilli, curry leaves]), 1/4 tsp turmeric, a pinch of asafoetida, 1/2 tsp salt, 2 cups buttermilk.

In a 2L Pressure Baker, layer as below:
Layer 1: 1/4 cup thin buttermilk
Layer 2: 1 cup chopped vegetables
Layer 3: PIP – spiced buttermilk mixture (see prep.)

Cook on high for 3 whistles or 5 minutes. Release pressure. Mix everything with 1 tsp bottled tadka.

Wednesday: No-coconut Morekuzhambu

Prep.: Soak 1 tbsp tuvar dal, 1/2 tbsp rice (optional), 1 tsp each (cumin, coriander seeds), 2 dry red chillies for 3 hours. Drain. Blend with 1/2 tsp salt, 1 tsp each (curry leaves, ginger), a pinch each (turmeric powder, asafoetida), 2 tbsp water to a thick paste. Mix in 1 cup buttermilk.

In a 2L Pressure Baker, layer as below:
Layer 1: 1/4 cup thin buttermilk
Layer 2: 1 cup chopped vegetables
Layer 3: PIP – spiced buttermilk mixture (see prep.)

Cook on high for 3 whistles or 5 minutes. Release pressure. Mix everything with 1/2 cup buttermilk, 1 tsp bottled tadka.

Thursday: Chettinad Morekuzhambu

Prep.: Soak 1tbsp each (chana dal, coriander seeds), 1tsp cumin, 2 dry red chillies for 30 minutes. Drain. Blend with 1/4 cup chopped coconut, 1tsp ginger, 1 green chilli, 1 garlic clove (optional), a pinch of turmeric powder, 1/4 cup buttermilk to a thick paste.

In a 2L Pressure Baker, layer as below:
Layer 1: 1tbsp coconut oil
Layer 2: 1/2 cup sliced onion
Layer 3: 1 cup chopped white pumpkin
Layer 4: PIP – spiced buttermilk mixture (see prep.)

Cook on high for 2 whistles or 5 minutes. Release pressure. Mix everything with 1 cup buttermilk, 1tsp bottled tadka.

Friday: Pathiya Morekuzhambu

Prep.: Soak for 30 minutes 1tbsp each (chana dal, coriander seeds, pepper). Blend with 1tsp ginger, a pinch each (turmeric powder, asafoetida), 1/4 cup buttermilk to a thick paste.

In a 2L Pressure Baker, layer as below:
Layer 1: 1tbsp coconut oil
Layer 2: 2 cups chopped spinach
Layer 3: Spice paste (see prep.)

Cook on high for 2 whistles or 5 minutes. Release pressure. Mix everything with 1 cup buttermilk, 1tsp bottled tadka.

Saturday: Paruppu Urundai Morekuzhambu

Prep.: Soak 1/2 cup tuvar dal for 1 hour. Drain. Blend with 3 dry red chillies, 1/4 cup chopped coconut, 3 curry leaves, 1tsp each (ginger, oil),

1/2tsp salt to a coarse paste. Shape into marble-sized balls. Blend 1/4 cup each (chopped coconut, buttermilk), 3 green chillies, 1tsp cumin, 1/2tsp salt to a smooth paste.

In a 2L Pressure Baker, layer as below:
Layer 1: 1/2 cup thin buttermilk
Layer 2: Lentil balls
Layer 3: PIP – spiced coconut paste (see prep.) mixed with 1 cup butter milk

Cook on high for 3 whistles or 5 minutes. Let pressure settle. Mix everything with 1tsp bottled tadka.

Sunday: Kalyana Morekuzhambu (Vadai/Papad/Bajji Morekuzhambu)

Prep.: Blend 1/2 cup chopped coconut, 4 green chillies, 1tsp each soaked (tuvar dal, rice [optional], coriander seeds, cumin seeds), 1/2tsp salt, 1/4tsp turmeric powder, 1/4 cup water to a thick paste.

In a 2L Pressure Baker, layer as below:
Layer 1: 1/2 cup buttermilk
Layer 2: PIP – spiced coconut paste (see prep.) mixed with 2 cups buttermilk.

Cook on high for 3 whistles or 5 minutes. Release pressure. Mix everything with 1/2 cup vada/bajji/crushed papad, 1tsp bottled tadka.

Common tadka:

Mustard seeds, fenugreek seeds and curry leaves.

TELUGU PAPPU (VEGETABLE–LENTIL STEW)

Base: Lentils
Flavouring: Oil, Bottled Tadka (p. 26)
Additives: Vegetables, Fruits, Herbs, Ghee (p. 27)

Monday: Classic Gatti Pappu

Prep.: Soak 1/4 cup masoor dal in water for 2 hours. Drain.

In a 2L Pressure Baker, layer as below:
Layer 1: 1tbsp ghee, 1/4 cup water
Layer 2: Dal, a pinch of turmeric powder

Cook on high for 4 whistles or 5 minutes. Let pressure settle. Mash with 1/2tsp salt. Mix in 1tbsp bottled tadka.

Tuesday: Dosakka Pappu

Prep.: Soak 1/4 cup tuvar dal in water for 4 hours. Drain.

In a 2L Pressure Baker, layer as below:
Layer 1: 1/4 cup water, 1tbsp oil
Layer 2: 1 cup chopped round yellow cucumber (dosakka)/any vegetable
Layer 3: Dal, 1/4tsp turmeric powder, a pinch of asafoetida

Cook on high for 4 whistles or 5 minutes. Let pressure settle. Mash with 1/2tsp salt. Mix in 1tbsp bottled tadka.

Wednesday: Palakoora Pappu

Prep.: Soak 1/4 cup moong dal in water for 2 hours. Drain.

In a 2L Pressure Baker, layer as below:
Layer 1: 1/4 cup water, 1tbsp oil
Layer 2: Dal, 1/4tsp turmeric powder, a pinch of asafoetida
Layer 3: PIP – 3 cups chopped spinach

Cook on high for 4 whistles or 5 minutes. Release pressure. Mash with 1/2tsp salt. Mix in 1tbsp bottled tadka.

Thursday: Tomato – Pachimirpakkaya Pappu

Prep.: Soak 1tbsp each dal (tuvar, chana, moong, masoor) in water for 4 hours. Drain.

In a 2L Pressure Baker, layer as below:
Layer 1: 1tbsp oil
Layer 2: 1.5 cup chopped tomato, 3 chopped green chillies
Layer 3: Dal, 1/4tsp turmeric powder, a pinch of asafoetida

Cook on high for 4 whistles or 5 minutes. Let pressure settle. Mash with 1/2tsp salt. Mix in 1tbsp bottled tadka.

Friday: Chinta Chiguru Pappu (Tamarind Leaves Dal)

Prep.: Soak 1/4 cup moong dal in water for 2 hours. Drain.

In a 2L Pressure Baker, layer as below:
Layer 1: 1/4 cup water, 1tbsp oil
Layer 2: 1 cup tender tamarind leaves (or sour spinach/fenugreek leaves)
Layer 3: Dal, 1/4tsp turmeric powder, a pinch of asafoetida

Cook on high for 4 whistles or 5 minutes. Let pressure settle. Mash with 1/2tsp salt. Mix in 1tbsp bottled tadka.

Saturday: Mixed Sprouts Pappu

In a 2L Pressure Baker, layer as below:
Layer 1: 1/4 cup water, 1tbsp ghee
Layer 2: 1/2 cup mixed sprouts, 1 chopped green chilli, 1tsp grated ginger, a pinch of turmeric powder

Cook on high for 4 whistles or 5 minutes. Let pressure settle. Mash with 1/2tsp salt. Mix in 1tbsp bottled tadka.

Sunday: Mamdikkaya Pappu

In a 2L Pressure Baker, layer as below:
Layer 1: 1/4 cup water, 1tbsp ghee
Layer 2: 1/2 cup chopped raw mango, 1 chopped green chilli, a pinch of turmeric powder
Layer 3: 1/2 cup cooked dal

Cook on high for 4 whistles or 5 minutes. Release pressure. Mash with 1/2tsp salt. Mix in 1tbsp bottled tadka.

Tips

- Serve as dips with roasted papads.
- Mix in 1/4 cup cooked rice, 1 cup water/stock and serve as a full-meal soup.
- Serve a small quantity of rice over Pappu and not the other way around.

TAMIL PARUPPU USILI (VEGETABLES WITH SPICED LENTIL CRUMBLE)

Base: Soaked Lentils, Vegetables
Flavouring: Chillies, Turmeric, Asafoetida, Bottled Tadka (p. 26)
Additives: Coconut, Herbs, Bottled Tadka

Monday: Classic Paruppu Usili

Prep.: Soak 1/2 cup chana dal for 4 hours. Drain. Add 3 dry red chillies, a pinch of turmeric powder and a pinch of asafoetida, 1/2tsp salt. Blend to a coarse paste. Shape into thin patties.

In a 2L Pressure Baker, layer as below:
Layer 1: 1/4 cup water, 1tsp oil
Layer 2: 2 cups chopped beans
Layer 3: Dal patties (see prep.)

Cook on high for 3 whistles or 5 minutes. Release pressure. Remove patties. Let cool and crumble/blend to a coarse powder. Mix with beans.

Tuesday: Masala Vada Usili

Prep.: Blend 4 pre-prepared masala vada to have 2 cups coarse powder.

In a 2L Pressure Baker, layer as below:
Layer 1: 1/4 cup water, 1tsp oil
Layer 2: 2 cups chopped cluster beans
Layer 3: Vada powder (see prep.)

Cook on high for 3 whistles or 5 minutes. Release pressure. Mix everything with 1tbsp bottled tadka.

Wednesday: Paruppu Podi Usili

Prep.: Blend 1 cup roasted gram, 4 green chillies, a pinch each (turmeric powder, asafoetida), 1/2tsp salt. Mix with 1tbsp water to a coarse paste. Shape into small loose balls.

In a 2L Pressure Baker, layer as below:
Layer 1: 1/4 cup water, 1tsp oil
Layer 2: 3 cup sundakkai (Turkey berries)
Layer 3: Lentil balls

Cook on high for 3 whistles or 5 minutes. Release pressure. Remove balls. Let cool and crumble/blend to a coarse powder. Use a masher to crush sundakkai. Mix everything.

Thursday: Palaparuppu Usili

Prep.: Soak overnight 2tbsp each dal (chana, tuvar, moong, masoor, urad). Drain. Add 3 red chillies, a pinch each (turmeric powder, asafoetida), 1/2tsp salt. Blend to a coarse paste. Shape into thin loose patties.

In a 2L Pressure Baker, layer as below:
Layer 1: 1/4 cup water, 1tsp oil
Layer 2: 4 cups chopped banana flower
Layer 3: Lentil patties

Cook on high for 3 whistles or 5 minutes. Release pressure. Remove patties. Let cool and crumble/blend to a coarse powder. Mix everything.

Friday: Sprouts Usili

Prep.: Take 1 cup mixed sprouts. Add 3 red chillies, a pinch each (turmeric powder, asafoetida), 1/2tsp salt. Blend to a coarse paste. Shape into thin patties.

In a 2L Pressure Baker, layer as below:
Layer 1: 2tbsp water, 1tsp oil
Layer 2: 4 cups capsicum cut big
Layer 3: Lentil patties

Cook on high for 2 whistles or 4 minutes. Release pressure. Remove patties. Let cool and crumble/blend to a coarse powder. Mix everything.

Saturday: Appala Usili

Prep.: Take 8 roasted papads. Crush to have 1 cup coarse powder. Add 3 finely chopped green chillies, a pinch each (turmeric powder, asafoetida), 1/2tsp salt. Add 1/4 cup water and shape into small balls.

In a 2L Pressure Baker, layer as below:
Layer 1: 2tbsp water, 1tsp oil
Layer 2: 250g chopped cabbage
Layer 3: Papad powder
Layer 4: 3 finely chopped green chillies, a pinch each (turmeric powder, asafoetida), 1/2tsp salt

Cook on high for 2 whistles or 4 minutes. Release pressure. Mix everything.

Sunday: Marathi Watli Dal

Prep.: Soak 1/2 cup chana dal for 4 hours. Drain. Add 4 green chillies, a pinch each (turmeric powder, asafoetida), 1/2tsp salt. Blend to a coarse paste. Shape into small marble-sized balls.

In a 2L Pressure Baker, add 1/2 cup water. Place the inner vessel with the balls of dal. Cook on high for 6 whistles or 7 minutes. Let pressure settle. Let cool and crumble/blend to a coarse powder. Mix with 1/4 cup grated coconut, 1tsp bottled tadka.

Tip

Blend soaked and drained dal in brief pulses for a coarse texture.

MUMBAI PAV BHAJI (SPICED VEGETABLE MASH)

Base: Starchy Vegetables, Animal/Plant Protein, Fat (Butter/Oil) and Micronutrients (Vegetables)
Flavouring: Pav Bhaji Masala/Garam Masala Powder, Ginger-garlic Paste (p. 28)
Additives: Cheese, Paneer, Chopped Onions, Lemon Juice, Caramelized Onion/Tomato (p. 29)

Monday: Classic Pav Bhaji

In a 2L Pressure Baker, layer as below:
Layer 1: 3tbsp butter, 1tbsp water
Layer 2: 1/2 cup each chopped (onion, tomato) arranged in a bull's-eye method
Layer 3: 1/2 cup each chopped (potato, beans, carrot)
Layer 4: 1/4 cup each (beetroot, peas) mixed with 1tsp ginger-garlic paste, 1/2tsp each (salt, chilli powder, garam masala powder)

Cook on high for 2 whistles or 6 minutes. Release pressure. Mash and serve.

Tips

- Mix in grated cheese/paneer for Cheese/Paneer Pav Bhaji.
- Do not mash for Khada Pav Bhaji.

Tuesday: Low-fat Pav Bhaji

In a 2L Pressure Baker, layer as below:
Layer 1: 1/4 cup water
Layer 2: 1/2 cup each chopped (potato, beans, carrot)
Layer 3: 1tbsp each (caramelized onion, tomato)
Layer 4: 1/4 cup each (beetroot, peas) mixed with 1tsp ginger-garlic paste, 1/2tsp each (salt, chilli powder, garam masala powder)

Cook on high for 2 whistles or 5 minutes. Release pressure. Mash and serve.

Wednesday: Jain/Vegan Pav Bhaji

In a 2L Pressure Baker, layer as below:
Layer 1: 1/4 cup water
Layer 2: 1/2 cup each chopped (raw banana, sweet corn, beans)
Layer 3: PIP – 1/2 cup each (peas, chopped capsicum) mixed with 1tbsp caramelized tomato, 1/2tsp each (salt, chilli powder, garam masala powder), 2tbsp almond powder.

Cook on high for 2 whistles or 5 minutes. Release pressure. Mash with 2tbsp butter (skip for vegan).

Thursday: Mushroom Pav Bhaji

In a 2L Pressure Baker, layer as below:
Layer 1: 2tbsp butter
Layer 2: 1 cup thinly sliced mushrooms
Layer 3: 1/2 cup each chopped (potato, beans, carrot)
Layer 4: 1/4 cup each (chopped beetroot, peas) mixed with 1tsp ginger-garlic paste, 1/2tsp each (salt, chilli powder, garam masala powder)

Cook on high for 2 whistles or 5 minutes. Release pressure. Mash. Mix in 1/2tsp lemon juice.

Friday: Kheema/Paleo Pav Bhaji

In a 2L Pressure Baker, layer as below:
Layer 1: 3tbsp butter
Layer 2: 1 cup minced meat
Layer 3: 1tbsp each caramelized (onion, tomato)
Layer 4: PIP – 1/2 cup each chopped (cauliflower, broccoli, capsicum), mixed with 1tsp ginger-garlic paste, 1/2tsp each (salt, chilli powder, garam masala powder)

Cook on high for 4 whistles or 6 minutes. Release pressure. Mash and serve.

Saturday: Anda Pav Bhaji

In a 2L Pressure Baker, layer as below:
Layer 1: 1/4 cup water
Layer 2: 1/2 cup each chopped (potato, beans, carrot)
Layer 3: 1tbsp each caramelized (onion, tomato)
Layer 4: 1/4 cup each (chopped beetroot, peas) mixed with 1tsp each (ginger-garlic paste, pepper powder), 1/2tsp each (salt, garam masala powder)
Layer 5: 2 well-washed eggs

Cook on high for 2 whistles or 6 minutes. Release pressure. Remove eggs and let cool. Mash vegetables. Mix in peeled and quartered eggs.

Sunday: Sprouts Pav Bhaji

In a 2L Pressure Baker, layer as below:
Layer 1: 1/4 cup water
Layer 2: 1/2 cup each (potato, mixed sprouts, carrot)
Layer 3: 1tbsp each caramelized (onion, tomato), 2 chopped green chillies
Layer 4: PIP – green peas, 1tsp ginger-garlic paste, 1/2tsp salt, 1/4tsp garam masala powder

Cook on high for 2 whistles or 6 minutes. Release pressure. Mash and serve.

Tips

- Chop potato into small pieces.
- Can use a hand blender briefly to mash.

KANNADIGA SAAGU (VEGETABLE–COCONUT STEW)

Base ingredients: Vegetables, Coconut
Flavouring: Garam Masala, Ginger, Bottled Tadka (p. 26)
Additives: Caramelized Onion/Tomato (p. 29), Milk, Cream, Yogurt, Water, Stock (p. 53-54), Coconut Milk, Other Plant Milk or any edible liquid of your choice

Monday: Classic White Saagu (Saatvik, Vegan)

Prep.: Blend 1/4 cup chopped coconut, 1tbsp roasted gram, 1tsp each (ginger, pepper, oil), 1/2tsp salt, 1 green chilli, 2tbsp water to a paste.

In a 2L Pressure Baker, layer as below:
Layer 1: 1/4 cup water
Layer 2: 1/2 cup each chopped (carrot, beans, potato)
Layer 3: Spiced coconut paste (see prep.)

Cook on high for 3 whistles or 5 minutes. Release pressure. Mix in 1/2 cup water/stock.

Tuesday: Masala Saagu

Prep.: Blend 1/4 cup chopped coconut, 1tbsp each (roasted gram, caramelized [onion and tomato]), 1tsp each (ginger-garlic paste, oil), 1/2tsp each (salt, garam masala powder), 2 green chillies, 2tbsp water to a paste.

In a 2L Pressure Baker, layer as below:
Layer 1: 1/4 cup water
Layer 2: 1/2 cup each chopped (carrot, beans, potato)
Layer 3: Spiced coconut paste (see prep.)

Cook on high for 3 whistles or 5 minutes. Release pressure. Mix in 1/2 cup water/stock.

Tuesday: Potato Batani Saagu (Coconut-free Saagu)

In a 2L Pressure Baker, layer as below:
Layer 1: 1/4 cup water
Layer 2: 1 cup potatoes chopped small
Layer 3: PIP – 1 cup fresh green peas, 1tbsp each caramelized (onion, tomato), 1tsp (ginger-garlic paste, oil), 1/2tsp each (chilli powder, salt, garam masala powder), a pinch each (turmeric powder, asafoetida)

Cook on high for 3 whistles or 5 minutes. Release pressure. Remove inner vessel. Mash potatoes. Mix everything with 1tsp lemon juice, 1tbsp chopped cilantro.

Wednesday: Mysore Saagu

Prep.: Blend 1/4 cup chopped coconut, 1tbsp each (roasted gram, caramelized onion, soaked poppy seeds, cilantro), 1tsp oil, 1/2tsp salt, 2 green chillies, 2tbsp water to a paste.

In a 2L Pressure Baker, layer as below:
Layer 1: 1/4 cup water
Layer 2: 1/2 cup each chopped (carrot, beans, potato), 5 curry leaves
Layer 3: Spiced coconut paste (see prep.)

Cook on high for 3 whistles or 5 minutes. Release pressure. Mix in 1/2 cup water/stock, 1tsp mustard bottled tadka.

Thursday: Green Saagu

Prep.: Blend 1/4 cup each chopped (coconut, cilantro), 1tbsp each roasted (gram, mint), 1tsp each (ginger, oil), 1/2tsp salt, 2 green chillies, 2tbsp water to a paste.

In a 2L Pressure Baker, layer as below:
Layer 1: 1/4 cup water
Layer 2: 1/2 cup each chopped (carrot, beans, potato), 5 curry leaves
Layer 3: Spiced coconut paste (see prep.)

Cook on high for 3 whistles or 5 minutes. Release pressure. Mix in 1/2 cup water/stock.

Friday: Red Saagu

Prep.: Blend 1/4 cup chopped coconut, 3 soaked and drained bydagi chillies, 1/2tsp each (Kashmiri chilli powder, salt), 2tbsp caramelized tomato, 1tbsp roasted gram, 1tsp each (ginger, oil), 1/4 cup water to a paste.
In a 2L Pressure Baker, layer as below:
Layer 1: 1/4 cup water
Layer 2: 1/2 cup each chopped (carrot, beans, potato), 5 curry leaves
Layer 3: Spiced coconut paste (see prep.)

Cook on high for 3 whistles or 5 minutes. Release pressure. Mix in 1/2 cup water/stock.

Saturday: Mixed Sprouts Saagu

Prep.: Blend 1/4 cup chopped coconut, 2tbsp roasted gram, 1tsp each (ginger, pepper powder, oil), 1/2tsp salt, 1 green chilli, 1/4tsp turmeric powder, 2tbsp water to a paste.

In a 2L Pressure Baker, layer as below:
Layer 1: 1/4 cup water

Layer 2: 2 cups mixed sprouts
Layer 3: Spiced coconut paste (see prep.)

Cook on high for 3 whistles or 5 minutes. Release pressure. Mix in 1/2 cup water.

Tip

If spice paste is not thick, use PIP.

MARATHI ZUNKA (SPICED VEGETABLE-GRAM FLOUR CRUMBLE)

Base: Gram Flour, Vegetables
Flavouring: Spices, Bottled Tadka (p. 26)
Additives: Spring Onion, Cilantro, Lemon Juice

Monday: Classic Zunka

Prep.: Mix 1/2 cup roasted gram flour with 1/4tsp each (chilli powder, salt, cumin powder, sugar), a pinch each (turmeric powder, asafoetida).

In a 2L Pressure Baker, layer as below:
Layer 1: 2tbsp oil
Layer 2: 1 cup chopped onion/2 cups chopped spring onion
Layer 3: Spiced gram flour (see prep.)

Cook on high for 3 whistles or 4 minutes. Release pressure. Mix everything with 1tsp bottled tadka.

Tuesday: Methi/Palak Zunka

Prep.: Mix 1/2 cup roasted gram flour with 1/4tsp each (chilli powder, salt, cumin powder, sugar), a pinch each (turmeric powder, asafoetida).

In a 2L Pressure Baker, layer as below:
Layer 1: 2tbsp oil
Layer 2: 1 cup chopped onion

Layer 3: 1 cup chopped fenugreek/mustard greens/spinach/kale
Layer 4: Spiced gram flour (see prep.)

Cook on high for 3 whistles or 4 minutes. Release pressure. Mix everything with 1tsp bottled tadka.

Wednesday: Capsicum/Cabbage Zunka

Prep.: Mix 1 cup roasted gram flour with 1/2tsp each (chilli powder, salt, cumin powder, sugar), a pinch each (turmeric powder, asafoetida)

In a 2L Pressure Baker, layer as below:
Layer 1: 2tbsp oil, 1tbsp water
Layer 2: 2 cups chopped capsicum/cabbage
Layer 3: Spiced gram flour (see prep.)

Cook on high for 1 whistle or 3 minutes. Release pressure. Mix everything with 1tsp bottled tadka.

Thursday: Tomato Zunka

Prep.: Mix 1 cup roasted gram flour with 1/2tsp each (salt, chilli powder, cumin powder, sugar), a pinch each (turmeric powder, asafoetida).

In a 2L Pressure Baker, layer as below:
Layer 1: 2tbsp oil
Layer 2: 1 cup each chopped (onion, tomato)
Layer 3: PIP – spiced gram flour (see prep.) mixed with 1tbsp water

Cook on high for 6 minutes. Release pressure. Mix everything with 1tsp bottled tadka, 1/4 cup chopped spring onion.

Friday: Sprouts Zunka

Prep.: Mix 1 cup roasted gram flour with 1/2tsp each (chilli powder, salt, cumin powder, sugar), a pinch each (turmeric powder, asafoetida).

In a 2L Pressure Baker, layer as below:
Layer 1: 1/4 cup water
Layer 2: 2 cups mixed sprouts
Layer 3: Spiced gram flour (see prep.)

Cook on high for 2 whistles or 4 minutes. Let pressure settle. Mix everything with 1tsp bottled tadka.

Saturday: Mushroom Zunka

Prep.: Mix 1 cup roasted gram flour with 1/2tsp each (chilli powder, salt, cumin powder, sugar, garam masala powder), a pinch each (turmeric powder, asafoetida).

In a 2L Pressure Baker, layer as below:
Layer 1: 1tbsp ghee
Layer 2: 2 chopped green chillies, 1 chopped garlic clove, 1tsp grated ginger
Layer 3: 2 cups chopped mushroom
Layer 4: Spiced gram flour (see prep.)
Layer 5: 1 cup chopped mushroom

Cook on high for 4 whistles or 5 minutes. Release pressure. Mix everything with 1tsp bottled tadka.

Sunday: Cauliflower/Broccoli Zunka

Prep.: Mix 1 cup roasted gram flour with 1/2tsp each (chilli powder, salt, cumin powder, sugar), a pinch each (turmeric powder, asafoetida).

In a 2L Pressure Baker, layer as below:
Layer 1: 3tbsp water
Layer 2: 250g cauliflower/broccoli florets
Layer 3: PIP – spiced gram flour (see prep.) mixed with 1tbsp water

Cook on high for 1 whistle or 4 minutes. Release pressure. Mix everything with 1tsp bottled tadka.

Tip

Ensure gram flour does not touch the base. If in doubt, add it in an inner vessel.

ODIYA BESARA (MUSTARD STEW)

Base: Mustard-garlic Sauce
Flavouring: Spices, Bottled Tadka (p. 26), Mustard Oil
Additives: Caramelized Onion/Tomato (p. 29), Vegetables, Seafood, Spinach, Egg, Meat

Monday: Pariba Ambula Besara (Mixed Vegetable Besara)

Prep.: Soak 2tbsp roasted mustard in water for 2 hours. Drain. Blend to a paste with 5 garlic cloves, 1tbsp cumin, 2 green chillies, 1/2tsp salt, 1tsp oil.

In a 2L Pressure Baker, layer as below:
Layer 1: 1/4 cup water
Layer 2: 2 dried mango pieces (10g)
Layer 3: 2 cups chopped mixed vegetables (potato, tomato, ridge gourd, squash, brinjal, carrot, cauliflower), 1tbsp caramelized onion
Layer 4: Mustard paste (see prep.)

Cook on high for 3 whistles or 6 minutes. Release pressure. Mix everything.

Tuesday: Palanga Besara (Spinach Besara)

Prep.: Soak 2tbsp roasted mustard in water for 2 hours. Drain. Blend to a paste with 5 garlic cloves, 1tbsp cumin, 2 green chillies, 1/2tsp salt, 1tsp oil.

In a 2L Pressure Baker, layer as below:
Layer 1: 1/4 cup water
Layer 2: 1 cup potato chopped small
Layer 3: 4 cups chopped spinach
Layer 4: Mustard paste (see prep.)

Cook on high for 3 whistles or 6 minutes. Release pressure. Mix everything with 1/4 cup water, 1tbsp bottled tadka.

Wednesday: Khatta Besara (Sour Besara)

Prep.: Soak 2tbsp roasted mustard in water for 2 hours. Drain. Blend to a paste with 5 garlic cloves, 1tbsp cumin, 2 green chillies, 1/2tsp salt, 1tsp oil.

In a 2L Pressure Baker, layer as below:
Layer 1: 2tbsp oil
Layer 2: 1 cup chopped tomato
Layer 3: 2 cups chopped mixed vegetables (potato, tomato, ridge gourd, squash, brinjal, carrot, cauliflower)
Layer 4: Mustard paste (see prep.)

Cook on high for 3 whistles or 6 minutes. Release pressure. Mix everything with 1/4 cup whisked yogurt.

Thursday: Anda Besara (Egg Besara)

Prep.: Soak 2tbsp roasted mustard in water for 2 hours. Drain. Blend to a paste with 5 garlic cloves, 1tbsp cumin, 2 green chillies, 1/2tsp salt, 1tsp oil.

In a 2L Pressure Baker, layer as below:
Layer 1: 2tbsp mustard oil
Layer 2: 1/2 cup each chopped (onion, tomato)
Layer 3: 1 cup potato chopped small
Layer 4: Mustard paste (see prep.)
Layer 5: 2 well-washed eggs

Cook on high for 4 whistles or 6 minutes. Let pressure settle. Peel and halve eggs. Mix everything.

Friday: Poi Chingudi Besara (Prawn–Spinach Besara)

Prep.: Soak 2tbsp roasted mustard in water for 2 hours. Drain. Blend to a paste with 1tbsp ginger-garlic paste, 1tsp each (cumin, oil), 2 dry red chillies, 1/2tsp salt.

In a 2L Pressure Baker, layer as below:
Layer 1: 2tbsp mustard oil
Layer 2: 125g prawns mixed with 1/2tsp salt, 1/4tsp turmeric powder
Layer 3: 1 cup chopped mixed vegetables (potato, tomato, ridge gourd, squash, brinjal)
Layer 4: 2 cups chopped spinach mixed with mustard paste (see prep.).

Cook on high for 3 whistles or 5 minutes. Release pressure. Mix everything.

Saturday: Macha Besara (Fish Besara)

Prep.: Soak 2tbsp roasted mustard in water for 2 hours. Drain. Blend to a paste with 1tbsp ginger-garlic paste, 1 green chilli, 1/2tsp salt, 1tsp oil.

In a 2L Pressure Baker, layer as below:
Layer 1: 2tbsp mustard oil
Layer 2: 250g chopped fish mixed with 1/2tsp salt, 1/4tsp turmeric powder
Layer 3: 1/2 cup each chopped small (potato, tomato)
Layer 4: PIP – 1tbsp caramelized onion, mustard paste (see prep.)

Cook on high for 3 whistles or 6 minutes. Release pressure. Mix mustard paste with 1/4 cup yogurt. Pour over fish and serve.

Sunday: Mangsha Besara (Mutton Besara)

Prep.: Mix 250g mutton chopped small with 1/4tsp each (turmeric powder, salt), 1tsp mustard oil. Soak 2tbsp roasted mustard in water for 2 hours. Drain. Blend to a paste with 5 garlic cloves, 2 green chillies, 1/2tsp salt, 1tsp each (amchur, oil).

In a 2L Pressure Baker, layer as below:
Layer 1: 2tbsp mustard oil
Layer 2: Mutton
Layer 3: 1tbsp each caramelized (onion, tomato), mustard paste (see prep.)

Cook on high for 8 whistles or 7 minutes. Let pressure settle. Mix everything.

Common tadka:

Mustard seeds, cumin seeds, fennel seeds, fenugreek seeds, kalonji (nigella) seeds in mustard oil/ghee.

Tips

- Can mix in tamarind pulp/tomato/yogurt as souring agent.
- Can mix in roasted badis (sun-dried, spiced lentil dumplings).
- Can use any mustard variety you prefer.
- Can add panch phoran powder as a layer.
- Can add chopped cilantro, bottled tadka as garnish.
- Can mix in cooked dal.

ODIYA DALMA (VEGETABLE–LENTIL STEW)

Base: Dal, Native Vegetables
Flavouring: Bottled Tadka (p. 26), Spices, Ginger, Ghee, Edible Camphor, Bay Leaf, Mustard Oil
Additives: Caramelized Onion/Tomato (p. 29), Tamarind, Coconut, Meat/Seafood

Monday: Classic Dalma

In a 2L Pressure Baker, layer as below:
Layer 1: 1/4 cup water
Layer 2: 2 cups chopped mixed native vegetables (squash, pumpkin, raw banana, brinjal, broad beans, cluster beans, split drumstick, colocasia)

Layer 3: 1tsp each roasted (cumin powder, dry red chilli powder), a pinch each (turmeric powder, asafoetida), 1tsp grated ginger, 1/2tsp salt
Layer 4: 1 cup cooked dal (moong/tuvar/masoor/chana)

Cook on high for 2 whistles or 5 minutes. Release pressure. Mix everything with 1/2 cup water, 2tbsp grated coconut, 1tbsp bottled tadka.

Tuesday: Mixed Dal Dalma

Prep.: 1/4 cup each dal mixed (moong, tuvar, chana, masoor) in water for 4 hours. Drain.

In a 2L Pressure Baker, layer as below:
Layer 1: 1/2 cup water
Layer 2: Mixed dals
Layer 3: 2 cups chopped mixed native vegetables (squash, pumpkin, raw banana, brinjal, broad beans, cluster beans, split drumstick, colocasia), 1/2 cup mixed sprouts
Layer 4: 1/2 cup chopped tomato, 1tsp each roasted (cumin powder, dry red chilli powder, salt, grated ginger) a pinch each (turmeric powder, asafoetida), 1tbsp caramelized onion

Cook on high for 4 whistles or 6 minutes. Release pressure. Mix everything with 1/2 cup water, 1tbsp bottled tadka.

Wednesday: Habiso Dalma

In a 2L Pressure Baker, layer as below:
Layer 1: 1/4 cup water
Layer 2: 2 cups chopped mixed native vegetables (squash, pumpkin, raw jackfruit, brinjal, broad beans, cluster beans, split drumstick, colocasia)
Layer 3: 1tsp each (grated ginger, roasted cumin powder, salt), 2tsp pepper powder, a pinch of asafoetida
Layer 4: 1 cup cooked and mashed dal (moong/tuvar)

Cook on high for 2 whistles or 5 minutes. Release pressure. Mix everything with 1/2 cup water, 1 tbsp ghee.

Thursday: Palanga Dalma

In a 2L Pressure Baker, layer as below:
Layer 1: 1/4 cup water
Layer 2: 2 cups chopped mixed native vegetables (squash, pumpkin, raw banana, brinjal, broad beans, cluster beans, split drumstick, colocasia)
Layer 3: 2 cups chopped spinach
Layer 4: 1 tsp each roasted (salt, cumin powder, dry red chilli powder, grated ginger) a pinch each (turmeric powder, asafoetida)
Layer 5: 1 cup cooked dal (moong/tuvar/masoor/chana)

Cook on high for 2 whistles or 5 minutes. Release pressure. Mix everything with 1/2 cup water, 1 tbsp bottled tadka.

Friday: Chingudi Macha Dalma

In a 2L Pressure Baker, layer as below:
Layer 1: 2 tbsp mustard oil
Layer 2: 1/2 cup each chopped (prawns, fish)
Layer 3: 2 cups chopped mixed native vegetables (squash, pumpkin, raw banana, brinjal, broad beans, cluster beans, split drumstick, colocasia)
Layer 4: 2 cups chopped spinach
Layer 5: 1 tbsp caramelized onion, 1 tsp each roasted (cumin powder, dry red chilli powder, ginger-garlic paste), a pinch of turmeric powder, 1/2 tsp salt
Layer 6: 1/2 cup cooked dal (moong/tuvar/masoor/chana)

Cook on high for 2 whistles or 5 minutes. Release pressure. Mix everything with 1/2 cup water, 1 tbsp bottled tadka.

Saturday: Anda Dalma

In a 2L Pressure Baker, layer as below:

Layer 1: 1/4 cup water

Layer 2: 2 cups chopped mixed native vegetables (squash, pumpkin, raw banana, brinjal, broad beans, cluster beans, split drumstick, colocasia)

Layer 3: 1tsp each roasted (cumin powder, grated ginger, dry red chilli powder), a pinch each (turmeric powder, asafoetida), 1/2tsp salt

Layer 4: 1 cup cooked dal (moong/tuvar/masoor/chana)

Layer 5: 2 well-washed eggs

Cook on high for 2 whistles or 5 minutes. Release pressure. Remove egg. Mix everything with 1/2 cup water, 2tbsp grated coconut, 1tbsp bottled tadka. Let eggs cool. Peel, halve and mix in.

Sunday: Mutton Dalma

Prep.: Mix 250g mutton chopped small with 1/4 cup yogurt, 1/4tsp each (salt, turmeric powder, ginger-garlic paste, garam masala powder). Let rest for 30 minutes.

In a 2L Pressure Baker, layer as below:

Layer 1: 2tbsp mustard oil

Layer 2: 1/2 cup chopped tomato

Layer 3: Spiced mutton (see prep.)

Layer 4: PIP – 2 cups chopped mixed native vegetables (squash, pumpkin, raw banana, brinjal, broad beans, cluster beans, split drumstick, colocasia) mixed with 1tsp each roasted (cumin powder, dry red chilli powder), a pinch each (turmeric powder, asafoetida), 1tbsp caramelized onion, 1/2tsp salt

Cook on high for 8 whistles or 7 minutes. Let pressure settle. Mix everything with 1/2 cup water, 1 cup cooked dal, 1tbsp bottled tadka.

Common tadka:

Mustard seeds, cumin seeds, fennel seeds, fenugreek seeds, kalonji (nigella) seeds in mustard oil/ghee.

Tips

- Serve without diluting as Badia Dalma.
- Mix in 1tsp tamarind paste for a sour version.
- Garnish with cilantro.
- If you prefer dal with a bite, add soaked and drained dal (as in Tuesday: Mixed Dal Dalma) as a bottom layer.

BENGALI DALNA (CUMIN–GINGER-BASED STEW)

Base: Cumin-ginger-chilli Paste
Flavouring: Garlic, Spices, Bottled Tadka (p. 26), Mustard Oil
Additives: Vegetables, Seafood, Spinach, Egg

Monday: Niramish Dalna (Satvik Dalna)

Prep.: Blend 1/4 cup chopped coconut with 1tsp each (cumin, oil), 2tsp ginger, 1 chopped green chilli, 1/2tsp salt to a paste.

In a 2L Pressure Baker, layer as below:
Layer 1: 2tbsp ghee
Layer 2: 1 cup chopped tomato
Layer 3: 2 cups chopped vegetables (potato, tomato, ridge gourd, squash, brinjal, carrot, cauliflower)
Layer 4: Spiced coconut paste (see prep.)
Layer 5: 1/2tsp each (sugar, garam masala powder), 1/4tsp turmeric powder

Cook on high for 3 whistles or 5 minutes. Release pressure. Mix everything with 1/2 cup water.

Tuesday: Chhanar Dalna (Paneer Dalna)

Prep.: Crush 1tsp cumin, 2tsp ginger, 1 chopped green chilli, 1/2tsp salt to a paste.

In a 2L Pressure Baker, layer as below:
Layer 1: 2tbsp oil
Layer 2: 1 cup chopped tomato
Layer 3: 1 cup potato chopped small
Layer 4: Spice paste (see prep.)
Layer 5: PIP – 1 cup chopped paneer mixed with 1/2tsp each (sugar, garam masala powder), 1/4tsp turmeric powder

Cook on high for 3 whistles or 5 minutes. Release pressure. Mix everything with 1/2 cup water, 1tbsp bottled tadka.

Wednesday: Mixed Vegetable Dalna

Prep.: Crush 1tsp cumin, 2tsp ginger, 2 chopped green chillies, 1/2tsp salt to a paste.

In a 2L Pressure Baker, layer as below:
Layer 1: 1/4 cup water
Layer 2: 1 cup each chopped (potato, chopped mixed vegetables [ridge gourd, squash, brinjal, carrot, cauliflower])
Layer 3: Spice paste (see prep.), 1tbsp each caramelized (onion, tomato)
Layer 4: 1/2tsp each (sugar, garam masala powder), 1/4tsp turmeric powder

Cook on high for 3 whistles or 6 minutes. Release pressure. Mix everything with 1/2 cup water.

Thursday: Dhokar Dalna (Dal Patties Dalna)

Prep.: Soak 1/4 cup chana dal overnight. Drain. Blend to a thick paste with 1/2tsp each (cumin, salt), 1 dry red chilli. Form into small patties.

In a 2L Pressure Baker, layer as below:
Layer 1: 2tbsp mustard oil
Layer 2: 1/2 cup each chopped (onion, tomato)
Layer 3: 1 cup potato chopped small
Layer 4: Dal patties (see prep.)

Cook on high for 4 whistles or 6 minutes. Let pressure settle. Mix everything.

Friday: Palong Saaker Dalna (Spinach Dalna)

Prep.: Crush 1tsp cumin, 2tsp ginger, 1 chopped green chilli, 1/2tsp salt to a paste.

In a 2L Pressure Baker, layer as below:
Layer 1: 1/4 cup water, 1tbsp mustard oil
Layer 2: 1 cup potato chopped small
Layer 3: 4 cups chopped spinach
Layer 4: Spice paste (see prep.), 1/2 cup badis (pre-prepared sun-dried lentil dumplings)
Layer 5: 1/2tsp each (sugar, garam masala powder, coriander powder), 1/4tsp turmeric powder

Cook on high for 3 whistles or 5 minutes. Release pressure. Mix everything with 1/4 cup milk, 1tbsp bottled tadka.

Saturday: Dimer Dalna (Egg Dalna)

Prep.: Crush 1tsp cumin, 2tsp ginger, 1 chopped green chilli, 1/2tsp salt to a paste.

In a 2L Pressure Baker, layer as below:
Layer 1: 2tbsp oil
Layer 2: 1/2 cup each chopped (onion, tomato)
Layer 3: 1 cup potato chopped small
Layer 4: Spice paste (see prep.), 1/2tsp each (sugar, garam masala powder), 1/4tsp turmeric powder
Layer 5: 2 well-washed eggs

Cook on high for 2 whistles or 5 minutes. Let pressure settle. Remove eggs, allow them to cool and then split them. Mix everything.

Sunday: Chingrir Dalna (Prawn Dalna)

Prep.: Crush 1tsp cumin, 2tsp ginger, 1 chopped green chilli, 1/2tsp salt to a paste.

In a 2L Pressure Baker, layer as below:
Layer 1: 2tbsp oil
Layer 2: 250g cleaned prawns
Layer 3: 1 cup potato chopped small
Layer 4: Spice paste (see prep.), 1/2tsp each (sugar, garam masala powder), 1/4tsp turmeric powder

Cook on high for 3 whistles or 5 minutes. Release pressure. Mix everything.

Common tadka:

Mustard seeds, cumin seeds, fennel seeds, fenugreek seeds, kalonji (nigella) seeds in mustard oil/ghee.

Tips

- Can mash all coarsely.
- Can mix in roasted/fried badis (sun-dried, spiced lentil dumplings).
- Can mix in milk/coconut milk.
- Can add panch phoran powder as a layer.
- Can add chopped cilantro, bottled tadka as garnish.

VEGETABLE-BASED DRY CURRIES

Base: Vegetables, Spinach, Sprouts
Flavouring: Spices, Bottled Tadka (p. 26)
Additives: Coconut, Jaggery, Cooked Dal, Roasted Gram

Monday: Basic Dry Vegetable Curry

In a 2L Pressure Baker, layer as below:
Layer 1: 1/4 cup water
Layer 2: 2 cups chopped mixed vegetables
Layer 3: 1 chopped green chilli, 1/2tsp salt

Cook on high for 2 whistles or 5 minutes. Release pressure. Mix in 1tbsp bottled tadka.

Tuesday: Dal-based Vegetable Curry

Prep.: Soak 1/4 cup moong/masoor dal for 30 minutes. Drain.

In a 2L Pressure Baker, layer as below:
Layer 1: 1/4 cup water, 1tsp oil
Layer 2: Dal
Layer 3: 2 cups chopped vegetables/mixed vegetables
Layer 4: 2 chopped green chillies, 1/2tsp salt, a pinch each (asafoetida, turmeric powder)

Cook on high for 2 whistles or 5 minutes. Release pressure. Mix in 1tbsp bottled tadka.

Wednesday: Sprouts/Fresh Legume-based Dry Curry

In a 2L Pressure Baker, layer as below:
Layer 1: 1/4 cup water
Layer 2: 2 cups sprouts/mixed sprouts/fresh legumes
Layer 3: 1 chopped green chilli, 1/2tsp salt, a pinch of asafoetida

Cook on high for 3 whistles or 5 minutes. Release pressure. Mix in 1tbsp bottled tadka.

Thursday: Spinach-based Dry Curry

In a 2L Pressure Baker, layer as below:
Layer 1: 1/4 cup water
Layer 2: 4 cups chopped spinach
Layer 3: 1 chopped green chilli, 1/2tsp salt

Cook on high for 2 whistles or 5 minutes. Release pressure. Mix in 1tbsp bottled tadka.

Friday: Masala-based Dry Curry

In a 2L Pressure Baker, layer as below:
Layer 1: 2tbsp oil
Layer 2: 1/2 cup each chopped (onion, deseeded tomato)
Layer 3: 2 cups chopped mixed vegetables
Layer 4: 1 chopped green chilli, 1tsp ginger-garlic paste, 1/2tsp each (salt, cumin powder, coriander powder)
Layer 5: 1/4tsp favourite spice mix (optional)

Cook on high for 3 whistles or 5 minutes. Release pressure. Mix in 1tbsp bottled tadka.

Saturday: Pickle/Chutney/Thokku-based Dry Curry

In a 2L Pressure Baker, layer as below:
Layer 1: 1/4 cup water
Layer 2: 2 cups chopped mixed vegetables
Layer 3: 2tbsp pickle/chutney/thokku

Cook on high for 2 whistles or 5 minutes. Release pressure. Mix in 1tbsp bottled tadka.

Sunday: Stuffed Vegetable Curry

Prep.: Take 1/2 cup Spiced Lentil Powder (p. 31)/spiced coconut powder/ puliyogare powder/roasted gram flour/masala paneer. Stuff into 250g hollowed vegetables (ladyfinger, ivy gourd, brinjal, green chillies, tomato, parwal [pointed gourd]). Wipe spice powder off the surface of vegetables.

In a 2L Pressure Baker, layer as below:
Layer 1: 3tbsp oil
Layer 2: 250g stuffed vegetables

Cook on high for 2 whistles or 5 minutes. Release pressure.

Common tadka:

Mustard seeds, dry red chillies, curry leaves or cumin seeds, dry red chillies.

Tips

- Cut quick cooking vegetables big/thick and tough vegetables small/thin.
- Mix in grated coconut/cooked dal/crushed peanuts/roasted gram flour after cooking.
- Use tadka of your choice.
- If excess water is left, do not cook further to evaporate. Drain and mix in with stews/use as stock.

SRI LANKAN HODHI (SPICED STEW)

Base: Coconut Milk
Flavouring: Bottled Tadka (p. 26), Spices, Dried Fish, Pandan Leaves
Additives: Vegetables, Egg, Seafood

Monday: Classic Kiri Hodhi (White Curry Hodhi)

In a 2L Pressure Baker, layer as below:
Layer 1: 2tbsp oil, 1tbsp water
Layer 2: 2 each (chopped green chillies, pandan leaves), 5 curry leaves
Layer 3: 1 cup chopped onion, 1/2tsp salt, 1 garlic clove, 1/4tsp turmeric powder
Layer 4: PIP –1 cup coconut milk

Cook on high for 3 whistles or 5 minutes. Let pressure settle. Mix everything.

Tuesday: Elavalu Kiri Hodhi (Vegetables Hodhi)

In a 2L Pressure Baker, layer as below:
Layer 1: 2tbsp oil, 1tbsp water
Layer 2: 2 each (chopped green chillies, pandan leaves), 5 curry leaves
Layer 3: 1 cup chopped onion, 1 garlic clove, 1/2tsp salt, 1/4tsp turmeric powder
Layer 4: 1 cup chopped vegetables
Layer 5: PIP – 1 cup coconut milk

Cook on high for 3 whistles or 5 minutes. Release pressure. Mix everything.

Wednesday: Bittara Kiri Hodhi (Egg Hodhi)

In a 2L Pressure Baker, layer as below:
Layer 1: 2tbsp oil, 1tbsp water
Layer 2: 2 each (chopped green chillies, pandan leaves), 5 curry leaves
Layer 3: 1 cup chopped onion, 1 garlic clove, 1/2tsp salt, 1/4tsp turmeric powder
Layer 4: 2 well-washed eggs
Layer 5: PIP – 1 cup coconut milk

Cook on high for 3 whistles or 4 minutes. Let pressure settle. Remove eggs. Let cool. Peel and halve. Mix everything.

Thursday Malu Kiri Hodhi (Fish Hodhi)

Prep.: Mix 200g chopped fish with a pinch of turmeric powder, 1tsp ginger-garlic paste, 1/4tsp salt

In a 2L Pressure Baker, layer as below:
Layer 1: 2tbsp oil, 1tbsp water
Layer 2: 2 each (chopped green chillies, pandan leaves), 5 curry leaves

Layer 3: 1 cup chopped onion, 1 garlic clove, 1/4tsp turmeric powder, 1/2tsp salt
Layer 4: Spiced fish (see prep.)
Layer 5: PIP –1 cup coconut milk

Cook on high for 3 whistles or 4 minutes. Release pressure. Pour coconut milk over fish. Do not mix.

Friday: Isso Kiri Hodi (Prawn Hodhi)

Prep.: Mix 200g chopped prawns with a pinch of turmeric powder, 1tsp ginger-garlic paste, 1/4tsp salt.

In a 2L Pressure Baker, layer as below:
Layer 1: 2tbsp oil, 1tbsp water
Layer 2: 2 each (chopped green chillies, pandan leaves), 5 curry leaves
Layer 3: 1 cup chopped onion, 1 garlic clove, 1/2tsp salt, 1/4tsp turmeric powder
Layer 4: Spiced prawns (see prep.)
Layer 5: PIP – 1 cup coconut milk

Cook on high for 3 whistles or 4 minutes. Release pressure. Mix everything.

Saturday: Kukul Mas Hodhi (Chicken Hodhi)

Prep.: Mix 200g chopped chicken with a pinch of turmeric powder, 1tsp ginger-garlic paste, 1/4tsp salt, 1/2tsp garam masala powder.

In a 2L Pressure Baker, layer as below:
Layer 1: 2tbsp each (oil, water)
Layer 2: 2 each (chopped green chillies, pandan leaves), 5 curry leaves
Layer 3: 1 cup chopped onion, 1 garlic clove, 1/2tsp salt, 1/4tsp turmeric powder
Layer 4: Spiced chicken (see prep.)
Layer 5: PIP – 1 cup coconut milk

Cook on high for 5 whistles or 6 minutes. Let pressure settle. Mix everything.

Sunday: South Tamil Nadu Mappilai Sodhi (Son-in-Law Stew)

Prep.: Blend 1/4 cup chopped coconut, 2 green chillies, 1tbsp roasted gram, 1tsp each (cumin, salt, coconut oil), 2tbsp water to a thick paste.

In a 2L Pressure Baker, layer as below:
Layer 1: 1/4 cup water
Layer 2: 5 curry leaves, 1 cup chopped beans
Layer 3: 1 cup potato chopped small, 2 slit green chillies
Layer 4: 1 cup chopped carrot
Layer 5: PIP – 1/4 cup fresh green peas
Layer 6: Spiced coconut paste (see prep.)
Layer 7: 2tbsp cooked dal (optional)
Layer 8: 1tbsp caramelized onions (optional)

Cook on high for 2 whistles or 6 minutes. Release pressure. Mash potatoes coarsely. Mix in 1/2 cup each (coconut milk, water), 1tsp bottled tadka.

Common tadka:

Fenugreek seeds, garlic, cinnamon in coconut oil.

Tips

- Add umbalakada (Maldives fish – dried) for extra flavour.
- Mix in lemon juice/kokum/tamarind paste for a sour version.
- Instead of placing the coconut milk in PIP, mix in after cooking.
- Replace coconut milk with tamarind water to make Thambum Hodhi (Sour Stew).

KERALA PULISSERI (SOUR COCONUT STEW)

Base: Yogurt-coconut Sauce
Flavouring: Spices, Bottled Tadka, Ginger, Cumin
Additives: Vegetables

Monday: Classic Pulisseri

Prep.: Blend 1/2 cup chopped coconut, 2 green chillies, 1tsp each (ginger, cumin, oil), 1/2tsp salt, 1/4tsp turmeric powder, 1/4 cup water to a thick paste.

In a 2L Pressure Baker, layer as below:
Layer 1: 1/2 cup thin buttermilk
Layer 2: PIP – spiced coconut paste (see prep.)

Cook on high for 3 whistles or 5 minutes. Let pressure settle. Mix everything with 1/2 cup whisked yogurt, 1tsp bottled tadka.

Tuesday: Vegetable Pulisseri

Prep.: Blend 1/2 cup chopped coconut, 2 green chillies, 1tsp each (ginger, cumin, oil), 1 garlic clove, 1/2tsp salt, 1/4tsp turmeric powder, 1/4 cup water to a thick paste.

In a 2L Pressure Baker, layer as below:
Layer 1: 1/4 cup thin buttermilk
Layer 2: 2 cups chopped vegetables
Layer 3: PIP – spiced coconut paste (see prep.)

Cook on high for 3 whistles or 5 minutes. Release pressure. Mix everything with 1/2 cup whisked yogurt, 1tsp bottled tadka.

Wednesday: Spice-based Pulisseri

Prep.: Blend 1/2 cup chopped coconut, 2 green chillies, 1tsp each (ginger, cumin, oil), 1 garlic clove, 1/2tsp salt, 1/4tsp turmeric powder, 1/4 cup water to a thick paste.

In a 2L Pressure Baker, layer as below:
Layer 1: 2tbsp oil
Layer 2: 1/2 cup chopped shallots, 5 curry leaves, 2 garlic cloves, 3 chopped green chillies, 1tsp chopped ginger
Layer 3: PIP – spiced coconut paste (see prep.)

Cook on high for 3 whistles or 5 minutes. Release pressure. Mix everything with 1/2 cup whisked yogurt, 1tsp bottled tadka.

Thursday: Instant Pulisseri

Blend 1/2 cup chopped coconut, 2 green chillies, 1tsp each (ginger, cumin, oil), 1/2tsp salt, a pinch each (turmeric powder, fenugreek powder), 1/2 cup yogurt, 1tbsp coconut oil to a thick sauce. Mix in 1/2 cup hot water and 1tbsp bottled tadka.

Friday: Keerai Pulisseri

Prep.: Blend 1/2 cup chopped coconut, 2 green chillies, 1tsp each (ginger, cumin, oil), 1/2tsp salt, 1/4tsp turmeric powder, 1/4 cup water to a thick paste.

In a 2L Pressure Baker, layer as below:
Layer 1: 1/2 cup thin buttermilk
Layer 2: 4 cups chopped spinach
Layer 3: PIP – spiced coconut paste (see prep.)

Cook on high for 2 whistles or 4 minutes. Release pressure. Mix everything with 1/2 cup whisked yogurt, 1tsp bottled tadka.

Saturday: Paruppurunda Pulisseri

Prep.: Soak 1/4 cup each tuvar/moong/masoor/chana dal for 2 hours. Drain. Blend with 2 dry red chillies, 1/4 cup chopped coconut, 3 curry leaves, 1tsp each (ginger, oil), 1/2tsp salt to a coarse paste. Shape into marble-sized balls.

Blend 1/2 cup chopped coconut, 2 green chillies, 1tsp each (ginger, cumin, oil), 1/2tsp salt, 1/4tsp turmeric powder, 1/4 cup water to a thick paste.

In a 2L Pressure Baker, layer as below:
Layer 1: 1/4 cup buttermilk
Layer 2: 1 cup chopped vegetables
Layer 3: 1 cup lentil balls
Layer 4: PIP – spiced coconut paste (see prep.) mixed with 1 cup buttermilk

Cook on high for 3 whistles or 5 minutes. Let pressure settle. Mix everything with 1tsp bottled tadka.

Sunday: Pazha Pulisseri

Prep.: Blend 1/2 cup chopped coconut, 2 green chillies, 1tsp each (ginger, cumin, oil), 1 garlic clove, 1/2tsp salt, 1/4tsp turmeric powder, 1/4 cup water to a thick paste.

In a 2L Pressure Baker, layer as below:
Layer 1: 1/4 cup thin buttermilk
Layer 2: 2 cups chopped fruits (mango, banana, pineapple)
Layer 3: PIP – spiced coconut paste (see prep.)

Cook on high for 3 whistles or 5 minutes. Release pressure. Mix everything with 1/2 cup whisked yogurt, 1tsp bottled tadka.

Common tadka:

Mustard seeds, fenugreek seeds, dry red chillies, curry leaves in coconut oil.

Tips

- If coconut paste is thick, PIP is not needed.
- Can replace/supplement yogurt with other souring agents.
- Can replace chilli with pepper for a satvik version.
- Can use ready-made vada/bajji in Paruppurunda Pulisseri.

SOUTH INDIAN SAMBAR (SOUR LENTIL STEW)

Base: Dal, Vegetables, Souring Agent
Flavouring: Sambar Powder, Bottled Tadka (p. 26)
Additives: Herbs, Coconut

Monday: Classic Sambar

In a 2L Pressure Baker, layer as below:
Layer 1: 1/4 cup water, 1tbsp oil
Layer 2: 2 cups chopped vegetables (potato, white pumpkin, carrot, squash, brinjal, drumstick)
Layer 3: 2tsp sambar powder, 1tsp tamarind paste, 1/2tsp salt
Layer 4: 1/2 cup cooked tuvar dal

Cook on high for 2 whistles or 5 minutes. Release pressure. Mix in 1/2 cup water, 1tbsp bottled tadka.

Tuesday: Tiffin Sambar

In a 2L Pressure Baker, layer as below:
Layer 1: 1tbsp oil
Layer 2: 1/2 cup each chopped (shallots, tomato)
Layer 3: 1 cup chopped mixed vegetables (potato, carrot, squash, brinjal)
Layer 4: 1tsp each (tamarind paste, jaggery, sambar powder), 1/2tsp salt
Layer 5: 1/2 cup cooked moong dal

Cook on high for 2 whistles or 5 minutes. Release pressure. Mix in 1/2 cup water, 1tbsp bottled tadka.

Wednesday: Arachu Vitta Sambar

Prep.: Roast and blend 1/4 cup chopped coconut, 1tbsp coriander seeds, 1/2tbsp each (chana dal, pepper), 1/4tsp fenugreek, a pinch each (turmeric powder, asafoetida), 3 dry red chillies to a paste with 2tbsp water.

In a 2L Pressure Baker, layer as below:
Layer 1: 1/4 cup water, 1tbsp oil
Layer 2: 2 cups chopped vegetables (potato, white pumpkin, carrot, squash, brinjal, drumstick)
Layer 3: Spiced coconut paste (see prep.), 1tsp tamarind paste, 1/2tsp salt
Layer 4: 1/2 cup cooked tuvar dal

Cook on high for 2 whistles or 5 minutes. Release pressure. Mix in 1/2 cup water, 1tbsp bottled tadka.

Thursday: Kadamba Sambar/Kalyana Sambar

In a 2L Pressure Baker, layer as below:
Layer 1: 1tbsp oil
Layer 2: 1 cup chopped tomato
Layer 3: 2 cups mixed vegetables (white pumpkin, carrot, squash, brinjal, drumstick)
Layer 4: 1tbsp coconut paste, 2tsp sambar powder, 1tsp tamarind paste, 1/2tsp salt
Layer 5: 1/4 cup each cooked dal (tuvar, moong)

Cook on high for 2 whistles or 5 minutes. Release pressure. Mix in 1/2 cup water, 1tbsp bottled tadka.

Friday: Instant Sambar

In a 2L Pressure Baker, layer as below:
Layer 1: 1tbsp oil, 1/4 cup water
Layer 2: 2 cups chopped vegetable (potato, white pumpkin, carrots, squash, brinjal, drumstick)
Layer 3: 2tsp sambar powder, 1/2tsp salt, 1tsp tamarind paste
Layer 4: PIP – 2tbsp paruppu podi (spiced lentil powder) p. 31 mixed with 1/2 cup water

Cook on high for 2 whistles or 5 minutes. Release pressure. Mix everything.

Saturday: Keerai Sambar

In a 2L Pressure Baker, layer as below:
Layer 1: 1/4 cup water, 1tbsp oil
Layer 2: 4 cups chopped spinach
Layer 3: 2tsp sambar powder, 1tsp tamarind paste, 1/2tsp salt
Layer 4: 1/2 cup cooked tuvar dal

Cook on high for 2 whistles or 5 minutes. Release pressure. Mix in 1/2 cup water, 1tbsp bottled tadka.

Sunday: Shallot Sambar (Caramelized Sambar)

In a 2L Pressure Baker, layer as below:
Layer 1: 2tbsp oil
Layer 2: 2 cups small whole shallots, 1 small whole tomato
Layer 3: PIP – 2tsp sambar powder, 1/2tsp salt, 1/2 cup water

Cook on high for 4 whistles or 5 minutes. Let pressure settle. Mash tomato. Mix in 1/2 cup each (cooked dal, water), 1tbsp bottled tadka.

Tips

- Prefer roasted sambar powder.
- Cooked dal can be mixed in at the very end.

Sambar powder:

Roast 1/4 cup tuvar dal, 1tbsp each (chana dal, coriander seeds) 5 dry red chillies, 1/4tsp each (fenugreek, turmeric, asafoetida), 1tsp each (cumin, pepper). Blend to a powder.

SUKKE (MANGALORE DRY FRY)

Base: Coconut, Chillies, Tamarind
Flavouring: Spices, Bottled Tadka (p. 26)
Additives: Caramelized Onion (p. 27) Vegetables, Meat, Seafood
Sukke paste: Roast 6 bydagi chillies and blend with 1tsp each (coriander seed, tamarind paste), 6 curry leaves, 1 garlic clove, 1/2tsp salt, 2tbsp water to a fine paste.

Spiced coconut paste:

Blend 1/2 cup chopped coconut with 1tsp each (cumin, coconut oil), 1/2tsp salt, 1/4tsp turmeric, to a coarse paste.

Monday: Mixed Vegetable Sukke

In a 2L Pressure Baker, layer as below:
Layer 1: 1/4 cup water
Layer 2: 2 cups chopped non-watery vegetables, 1tbsp caramelized onion
Layer 3: Sukke paste

Cook on high for 2 whistles or 5 minutes. Release pressure. Mix everything with spiced coconut paste, 1tsp bottled tadka.

Tuesday: Sprouts/Spinach Sukke

In a 2L Pressure Baker, layer as below:
Layer 1: 1/4 cup water
Layer 2: 2 cups sprouts/4 cups chopped spinach
Layer 3: Sukke paste, 1tbsp caramelized onion

Cook on high for 2 whistles or 5 minutes. Release pressure. Mix everything with spiced coconut paste, 1tsp bottled tadka.

Wednesday: Soya/Paneer Sukke

In a 2L Pressure Baker, layer as below:
Layer 1: 1tbsp oil
Layer 2: 1/2 cup each chopped (onion, tomato)
Layer 3: Sukke paste, 1tbsp caramelized onion
Layer 4: PIP – soya/paneer

Cook on high for 3 whistles or 4 minutes. Release pressure. Mix everything with 1/2 cup water, 1tsp bottled tadka.

Thursday: Egg Sukke

In a 2L Pressure Baker, layer as below:
Layer 1: 2tbsp oil, 1tbsp water
Layer 2: 1 cup chopped onion
Layer 3: 4 well-washed eggs
Layer 4: PIP – sukke paste

Cook on high for 4 whistles or 5 minutes. Release pressure. Let eggs cool. Peel, chop and mix everything with spiced coconut paste, 1tsp bottled tadka.

Friday: Chicken Sukke

In a 2L Pressure Baker, layer as below:
Layer 1: 1tbsp oil
Layer 2: 250g chopped chicken mixed with 1tsp ginger-garlic paste, 1/2tsp salt, 1/4tsp turmeric powder
Layer 3: Sukke paste, 1tbsp caramelized onion

Cook on high for 5 whistles or 6 minutes. Release pressure. Mix everything with spiced coconut paste, 1tsp bottled tadka.

Saturday: Fish/Prawn Sukke

In a 2L Pressure Baker, layer as below:
Layer 1: 1tbsp oil
Layer 2: 250g chopped fish/prawns mixed with 1/2tsp salt, 1/4tsp turmeric powder
Layer 3: Sukke paste, 1tbsp caramelized onion

Cook on high for 3 whistles or 4 minutes. Release pressure. Mix everything with spiced coconut paste, 1tsp bottled tadka.

Sunday: Mutton Sukke

Layer 1: 2tbsp water, 1tbsp oil
Layer 2: 250g chopped boneless tender mutton mixed with 1/2tsp salt, 1/4tsp turmeric powder
Layer 3: Sukke paste, 1tbsp caramelized onion

Cook on high for 10 whistles or 7 minutes. Let pressure settle. Mix everything with coconut paste, 1tsp bottled tadka.

Common tadka:

Mustard, dry red chillies, onion, garlic in coconut oil.

Tips

- Can blend in cashew/other nuts for a richer masala.
- Keep sukke paste in an inner vessel if not too thick.
- Can use raw mango/kokum in place of tamarind.
- Salt and squeeze meats/sun dry them or leave them uncovered in the refrigerator to reduce their moisture content.

GASSI (MANGALORE COCONUT–CHILLI STEW)

Base: Coconut, Chillies
Flavouring: Spices, Bottled Tadka (p. 26)
Additives: Vegetables, Meat, Seafood, Egg
Gassi paste: Roast 6 bydagi chillies, 5 curry leaves, 1tsp each (cumin, coriander seeds, pepper), 1/2tsp fenugreek seeds. Blend with 1/4 cup chopped coconut, 1tsp each (Kashmiri chilli powder, garlic paste, tamarind paste, jaggery, sesame seeds, poppy seeds, coconut oil), 1tbsp caramelized onion, 1/2tsp each (salt, garam masala powder), 1/4 cup water to a thick paste. (Jaggery, garam masala powder, fenugreek, sesame, poppy seeds are optional.) Blend coarse for thick curry or smooth for gravy.

Monday: Mixed Vegetable Gassi

In a 2L Pressure Baker, layer as below:
Layer 1: 1/4 cup water
Layer 2: 2 cups chopped vegetables
Layer 3: 1/2 cup gassi paste

Cook on high for 2 whistles or 5 minutes. Release pressure. Mix everything with 1/4 cup coconut milk, 1tsp bottled tadka.

Tuesday: Sprouts/Spinach Gassi

In a 2L Pressure Baker, layer as below:
Layer 1: 1tbsp each (oil, water)
Layer 2: 2 cups sprouts/4 cups chopped spinach
Layer 3: Gassi paste

Cook on high for 2 whistles or 5 minutes. Release pressure. Mix everything with 1/2 cup water, 1tsp bottled tadka.

Wednesday: Soya/Paneer Gassi

In a 2L Pressure Baker, layer as below:
Layer 1: 2tbsp oil

Layer 2: 1/2 cup each chopped (onion, tomato)
Layer 3: PIP – gassi paste
Layer 4: PIP – 1 cup soya/paneer

Cook on high for 2 whistles or 4 minutes. Release pressure. Mix everything with 1/2 cup water, 1tsp bottled tadka.

Thursday: Egg Gassi

In a 2L Pressure Baker, layer as below:
Layer 1: 2tbsp oil
Layer 2: 1/2 cup each chopped (onion, tomato)
Layer 3: 4 well-washed eggs
Layer 4: PIP – gassi paste

Cook on high for 3 whistles or 5 minutes. Release pressure. Let eggs cool. Peel, chop and mix everything with 1/2 cup water, 1tsp bottled tadka.

Friday: Chicken Gassi

In a 2L Pressure Baker, layer as below:
Layer 1: 1tbsp oil
Layer 2: 250g chopped chicken mixed with 1tsp ginger-garlic paste, 1/2tsp salt, 1/4tsp turmeric powder
Layer 3: Gassi paste

Cook on high for 5 whistles or 6 minutes. Release pressure. Mix everything with 1/2 cup water, 1tsp bottled tadka.

Saturday: Fish/Prawn Gassi

In a 2L Pressure Baker, layer as below:
Layer 1: 1tbsp oil
Layer 2: 250g chopped fish/prawns mixed with 1tsp ginger-garlic paste, 1/2tsp salt, 1/4tsp turmeric powder
Layer 3: Gassi paste

Cook on high for 3 whistles or 4 minutes. Release pressure. Mix everything with 1/2 cup water, 1tsp bottled tadka.

Sunday: Mutton Gassi

Layer 1: 2tbsp water, 1tbsp oil
Layer 2: 250g chopped boneless tender mutton mixed with 1tsp ginger-garlic paste, 1/2tsp salt, 1/4tsp turmeric powder
Layer 3: 1 cup potato chopped big
Layer 4: PIP – gassi paste

Cook on high for 10 whistles or 7 minutes. Let pressure settle. Mix everything with 1/4 cup coconut milk and 1/4 cup water, 1tsp bottled tadka.

Common tadka:

Mustard seeds, dry red chillies, onion, garlic cloves in oil.

Tips

- Can blend in cashew/other nuts for a richer stew.
- Keep gassi paste in an inner vessel if not too thick.
- Can mix in caramelized onion, tomato.
- Can use kokum/raw mango in place of tamarind.
- Can garnish with fried onion.

JALFREZI (SPICY STIR-FRY)

Base: Onion, Tomato, Chillies
Flavouring: Spices, Bottled Tadka (p. 26)
Additives: Vegetables, Meats, Seafood, Eggs, Paneer

Monday: Vegetable-based Jalfrezi

In a 2L Pressure Baker, layer as below:
Layer 1: 1tbsp oil

Layer 2: 1/2 cup each chopped (onion, tomato) arranged in bull's-eye method, 1 slit green chilli

Layer 3: 2 cups bite-sized mixed vegetables mixed with 1tsp each (ginger-garlic paste, Kashmiri chilli powder), 1/2tsp each (cumin, coriander powder, garam masala powder, salt), a pinch of turmeric powder

Cook on high for 3 whistles or 5 minutes. Release pressure. Mix everything.

Tuesday: Sprouts-based Jalfrezi

In a 2L Pressure Baker, layer as below:

Layer 1: 1tbsp oil

Layer 2: 1/2 cup each chopped (onion, tomato) arranged in bull's-eye method, 1 slit green chilli

Layer 3: 2 cups sprouts mixed with 1tsp each (ginger-garlic paste, Kashmiri chilli powder), 1/2tsp each (cumin, coriander powder, garam masala powder, salt), a pinch of turmeric powder

Cook on high for 3 whistles or 5 minutes. Release pressure. Mix everything.

Wednesday: Cheese-based Jalfrezi

In a 2L Pressure Baker, layer as below:

Layer 1: 1tbsp oil

Layer 2: 1/2 cup each chopped (onion, tomato) arranged in bull's-eye method, 1 slit green chilli

Layer 3: PIP – 250g chopped paneer mixed with 1tsp each (ginger-garlic paste, Kashmiri chilli powder), 1/2tsp each (cumin, coriander powder, garam masala powder, salt), a pinch of turmeric powder

Cook on high for 3 whistles or 4 minutes. Release pressure. Mix everything.

Thursday: Egg-based Jalfrezi

In a 2L Pressure Baker, layer as below:
Layer 1: 1tbsp oil
Layer 2: 1/2 cup each chopped (onion, tomato), 1 slit green chilli
Layer 3: 1tsp each (ginger-garlic paste, Kashmiri chilli powder), 1/2tsp each (cumin, coriander powder, garam masala powder, salt), a pinch of turmeric powder
Layer 4: 2 well-washed eggs

Cook on high for 3 whistles or 4 minutes. Let pressure settle. Peel and chop eggs. Mix everything.

Friday: Poultry-based Jalfrezi

In a 2L Pressure Baker, layer as below:
Layer 1: 1tbsp oil
Layer 2: 1/2 cup each chopped (onion, tomato) arranged in bull's-eye method, 1 slit green chilli
Layer 3: 1 cup chopped chicken mixed with 1tsp each (ginger-garlic paste, Kashmiri chilli powder), 1/2tsp each (cumin, coriander powder, garam masala powder, salt), a pinch of turmeric powder

Cook on high for 5 whistles or 6 minutes. Release pressure. Mix everything.

Saturday: Meat-based Jalfrezi

In a 2L Pressure Baker, layer as below:
Layer 1: 2tbsp oil
Layer 2: 1/2 cup each chopped (onion, tomato) arranged in bull's-eye method, 1 slit green chilli
Layer 3: 1 cup mutton chopped small mixed with 1tsp each (ginger-garlic paste, Kashmiri chilli powder), 1/2tsp each (cumin, coriander powder, garam masala powder, salt), a pinch of turmeric powder

Cook on high for 10 whistles or 8 minutes. Let pressure settle. Mix everything.

Sunday: Seafood-based Jalfrezi

In a 2L Pressure Baker, layer as below:
Layer 1: 1tbsp oil
Layer 2: 1/2 cup each chopped (onion, tomato) arranged in bull's-eye method, 1 slit green chilli
Layer 3: 250g prawns/fish mixed with 1tsp each (ginger-garlic paste, Kashmiri chilli powder), 1/2tsp each (cumin, coriander powder, garam masala powder, salt), a pinch of turmeric powder

Cook on high for 3 whistles or 4 minutes. Release pressure. Mix everything.

Common tadka:

Green chillies, garlic cloves, onion in oil.

Tips

- Can mix in 1/2 cup finely chopped capsicum after cooking.
- Can vary spices to taste.
- Can mix in a liquid to convert the dry curry into a gravy.
- Chicken/prawn/fish can be salted and squeezed dry or kept uncovered in the refrigerator overnight or briefly sun-dried to remove excess moisture, which prevents onion caramelization. Else place them in an inner vessel and cook for a few more whistles.

KOFTA CURRY

Base: Vegetable, Meat, Dal, Paneer
Flavouring: Spices, Bottled Tadka (p. 26)
Additives: Cheese, Herbs, Dry Fruit, Nuts

Monday: Paneer Kofta

Grate 100g paneer. Mix in 1/4tsp each (salt, garam masala powder). Shape into loose balls.

Tuesday: Soya Kofta

Soak 1 cup soya chunks till soft. Blend with 2tbsp roasted gram flour, 1/4tsp each (salt, coriander powder, chilli powder, garam masala powder), a pinch of turmeric powder. Shape into small marble-sized balls.

Wednesday: Dal/Sprouts Kofta

Soak 1/2 cup dal for 4 hours. Drain. Or take 1 cup sprouts. Add 3 dry red chillies, a pinch each (turmeric powder, asafoetida), 1/2tsp salt. Blend dal/sprouts to a coarse paste. Shape into loose marble-sized balls.

Thursday: Vegetable Kofta

Take 1/4 cup each finely grated (carrot, potato, cauliflower, capsicum).
Mix in 1/4 cup grated (paneer/cheese), 2tbsp roasted gram flour, 1/4tsp each (salt, coriander powder, garam masala powder, chilli powder), a pinch of turmeric powder. Shape into small marble-sized balls.

Friday: Chicken/Mutton Kofta

Take 1 cup meat mince. Mix in 2tbsp wheat flour, 1tsp ginger-garlic paste, 1/4tsp each (salt, coriander powder, garam masala powder, chilli powder), a pinch of turmeric powder. Shape into small marble-sized balls.

Saturday: Nawabi Kofta

Blend 1/4 cup each (paneer, cashewnuts, raisins), 1 green chilli, 1/4tsp each (salt, cumin powder, garam masala powder). Shape into small, loose balls. Place on a sliced bread. Bring together edges to seal.

Sunday: Stuffed Kofta

Make small marble balls of any of the recipes above. Make larger lemon balls from another recipe. Seal the small ball inside the larger one. Prick all over with a fork.

Cooking Koftas:

For all the above, cook as follows:

In a 2L Pressure Baker, layer as below:
Layer 1: 2tbsp oil
Layer 2: 1/2 cup each chopped (onion, deseeded tomato), 2 chopped chillies
Layer 3: 1tbsp nut paste (see p. 80), 1tsp ginger-garlic paste, 1/2tsp each (cumin powder, garam masala powder), 1/4tsp each (salt, sugar)
Layer 4: Koftas

Cook on high for 4 whistles or 5 minutes. Release pressure (let pressure settle for meat-based koftas). Remove balls. Blend the rest. Mix everything.

Common tadka:

Bay leaves, cardamom, clove, cinnamon in ghee.

Tips

- Can mix in cream for Malai Kofta.
- Skip tomato for a white gravy.
- Can use corn flour as a binder.

DAL

Base: Dal
Flavouring: Spices
Additives: Vegetables, Bottled Tadka (p. 26), Spinach, Sprouts

Monday: Dhaba Dal

Prep.: Soak 1/2 cup moong/masoor/tuvar dal in water for 3 hours. Drain.

In a 2L Pressure Baker, layer as below:
Layer 1: 2tbsp oil
Layer 2: 1/2 cup each chopped (onion, tomato) arranged in bull's-eye method, 2 slit green chillies
Layer 3: Dal
Layer 4: 1tbsp kasuri methi, 1tsp ginger-garlic paste, 1/2tsp each (chilli powder, cumin powder, salt, garam masala powder), a pinch each (turmeric powder, asafoetida)

Cook on high for 5 whistles or 6 minutes. Let pressure settle. Mash everything with 1/2 cup water. Mix in 1tbsp bottled tadka.

Tuesday: Dal Palak

Prep.: Soak 1/2 cup moong/masoor dal in water for 3 hours. Drain.

In a 2L Pressure Baker, layer as below:
Layer 1: 1/4 cup water
Layer 2: 2 cups finely chopped spinach, 2 slit green chillies
Layer 3: Dal
Layer 4: 1tbsp kasuri methi, 1tsp each (ginger-garlic paste, chilli powder, cumin powder, salt, garam masala powder), a pinch each (turmeric powder, asafoetida)
Layer 5: 2 cups finely chopped spinach

Cook on high for 3 whistles or 5 minutes. Release pressure. Mash everything with 1/2 cup water. Mix in 1tbsp bottled tadka.

Wednesday: Vegetable Dal

Prep.: Soak 1/2 cup moong/masoor dal in water for 3 hours. Drain.

In a 2L Pressure Baker, layer as below:
Layer 1: 1/4 cup water
Layer 2: 1 cup of chopped vegetables, 2 slit green chillies
Layer 3: Dal
Layer 4: 1 cup chopped vegetables
Layer 5: 1tbsp kasuri methi, 1tsp ginger-garlic paste, 1/2tsp each (chilli powder, cumin powder, salt, garam masala), a pinch each (turmeric powder, asafoetida).

Cook on high for 3 whistles or 5 minutes. Release pressure. Mix everything with 1tbsp bottled tadka.

Thursday: Panchmela Dal

Prep.: Soak 2tbsp each dal (moong, masoor, chana, urad, tuvar) in water for 3 hours. Drain.

In a 2L Pressure Baker, layer as below:
Layer 1: 2tbsp ghee
Layer 2: 1 cup chopped tomato, 2 slit green chillies
Layer 3: Dal
Layer 4: 1tbsp kasuri methi, 1tsp ginger-garlic paste, 1/2tsp each (chilli powder, cumin powder, salt, garam masala powder), a pinch each (turmeric powder, asafoetida)

Cook on high for 5 whistles or 6 minutes. Let pressure settle. Mash everything with 1/2 cup water. Mix in 1tbsp bottled tadka.

Friday: Kosambari

Soak 1/4 cup split moong dal/chana dal in water for 2 hours. Drain. Mix in 1/4 cup grated coconut, 1 chopped green chilli, 1tsp lemon juice, 1/4tsp salt.

Saturday: Sprouted Dal Dry Curry

In a 2L Pressure Baker, layer as below:
Layer 1: 1/4 cup water
Layer 2: 2 cups dal sprouts, 2 slit green chillies
Layer 3: 1tbsp kasuri methi, 1tsp ginger-garlic paste, 1/2tsp each (chilli powder, cumin powder, salt, garam masala powder), a pinch each (turmeric powder, asafoetida)

Cook on high for 3 whistles or 5 minutes. Release pressure. Mix everything with 1tbsp bottled tadka.

Sunday: Watli Dal

Prep.: Soak 1/2 cup moong/masoor/tuvar/chana dal in water for 4 hours. Drain. Blend with 4 green chillies, 1/2tsp each (cumin, salt), a pinch each (turmeric powder, asafoetida) to a coarse paste.

In a 2L Pressure Baker, add 1 cup water, PIP – blended paste. Poke holes for steam to circulate.

Cook on high for 5 whistles or 6 minutes. Let pressure settle. Fluff up, break clumps. Mix in 1/4 cup grated coconut, 1tbsp each (bottled tadka, chopped cilantro, grated mango).

Common tadka:

Mustard seeds, cumin seeds, dry red chillies in oil.

Tips

- Mix in chopped roti bits to make Dal Dhokla.
- Mix in lemon juice/tamarind paste to make it Khatti Dal.
- Mix in caramelized onion/tomatoes (p. 27-28) to make Masala Dal.
- Mix in cream, nut paste to make Darbari Dal.

BENGALI POSTO

Base: Poppy Seed Paste
Flavouring: Mustard Oil
Additives: Caramelized Onion/Tomato (p. 29) Vegetables, Seafood, Fish, Egg, Meat
Posto paste 1: Soak 2tbsp poppy seeds in water for 2 hours. Drain. Blend 2 green chillies, 1/2tsp salt, 1/4tsp turmeric powder, 1tsp oil into a thick paste.
Posto paste 2: Soak 2tbsp poppy seeds in water for 2 hours. Drain. Blend 2 green chillies, 1/4tsp salt, 1tsp oil into a thick paste.

Monday: Aloo Potol Posto (Potato and Parwal in Poppy Seed Paste)

In a 2L Pressure Baker, layer as below:
Layer 1: 1tbsp each (oil, water)
Layer 2: 1 cup potato chopped small
Layer 3: 1 cup parwal chopped long in quarters
Layer 4: Posto paste 1

Cook on high for 2 whistles or 5 minutes. Release pressure. Mix everything.

Tuesday: Shaak Posto (Greens Posto)

In a 2L Pressure Baker, layer as below:
Layer 1: 2tbsp oil
Layer 2: 2 dried red chillies, 2 cups chopped edible greens (amaranth/spinach/Malabar spinach/any other greens)
Layer 3: PIP – posto paste 1

Cook on high for 2 whistles or 5 minutes. Release pressure. Mix everything.

Wednesday: Dim Posto (Egg Posto)

In a 2L Pressure Baker, layer as below:
Layer 1: 1/4 cup water
Layer 2: 4 well-washed eggs
Layer 3: PIP – posto paste 1
Layer 4: PIP – 2tbsp each caramelized (onion, tomato)

Cook on high for 2 whistles or 5 minutes. Let pressure settle. Drain water. Peel and halve the eggs. Mix everything with 1/4 cup water.

Thursday: Chingdi Posto (Prawn Posto)

In a 2L Pressure Baker, layer as below:
Layer 1: 2tbsp oil
Layer 2: 250g prawns marinated in 1/4tsp each (salt, turmeric powder)
Layer 3: PIP – posto paste 2

Cook on high for 3 whistles or 5 minutes. Release pressure. Mix everything.

Friday: Rui/Maach Posto (Fish Posto)

In a 2L Pressure Baker, layer as below:
Layer 1: 2tbsp mustard oil
Layer 2: 250g fish marinated in 1/4tsp each (salt, turmeric powder)

Layer 3: PIP – posto paste 2
Layer 4: 2tbsp caramelized onion

Cook on high for 2 whistles or 5 minutes. Release pressure. Mix gently.

Saturday: Murghi Posto (Chicken Posto)

In a 2L Pressure Baker, layer as below:
Layer 1: 2tbsp mustard oil
Layer 2: 250g chopped chicken marinated in 1tsp ginger-garlic paste, 1/4tsp each (turmeric powder, salt)
Layer 3: PIP – posto paste 2
Layer 4: 1tbsp each caramelized (onion, tomato)

Cook on high for 5 whistles or 6 minutes. Release pressure. Mix everything.

Sunday: Mangsho Posto (Mutton Posto)

Prep.: Soak 2tbsp poppy seeds in water for 2 hours. Drain. Blend 2 green chillies, 1/4tsp salt, 1tsp oil into a thick paste.

In a 2L Pressure Baker, layer as below:
Layer 1: 2tbsp mustard oil
Layer 2: 250g tender mutton chopped small marinated in 1/4tsp each (salt, turmeric powder), 1tsp ginger-garlic paste
Layer 3: PIP – posto paste 2
Layer 4: 2tbsp each caramelized (onion, tomato)

Cook on high for 8 whistles or 8 minutes. Let pressure settle. Mix everything.

Tips

- Can use any posto variety you prefer (black or white).
- Soaking of the posto is optional but preferred.

- Can add whole garam masalas.
- Can take the basic posto template and add 1tbsp chopped raw onion, 1tsp each chopped (green chillies, mustard oil). This 'Posto Bata' can be enjoyed on its own. It also pairs very well with hot rice/side dishes.

LAUNJI (WEST INDIAN SWEET AND SOUR STEW)

Base: Sweetener, Souring Agent
Flavouring: Spices, Bottled Tadka (p. 26)
Additives: Vegetables, Fruits, Sprouts

Monday: Fruit-based Launji

In a 2L Pressure Baker, layer as below:
Layer 1: 2tbsp oil
Layer 2: 2 cups chopped fruits (mango/tomato/grapes/pineapple)
Layer 3: 1 cup sugar, 1tsp amchur
Layer 4: 1/2tsp each (chilli powder, salt), a pinch of turmeric powder

Cook on high for 2 whistles or 5 minutes. Release pressure. Mix in 1tbsp bottled tadka.

Tuesday: Vegetable-based Launji

In a 2L Pressure Baker, layer as below.
Layer 1: 1/4 cup water
Layer 2: 2 cups chopped vegetables
Layer 3: 1tsp each (ginger-garlic paste, tamarind paste), 2tbsp jaggery
Layer 4: 1/2tsp each (chilli powder, salt), 1/4tsp garam masala powder, a pinch of turmeric powder

Cook on high for 2 whistles or 5 minutes. Release pressure. Mix in 1tbsp bottled tadka.

Wednesday: Sprout-based Launji

In a 2L Pressure Baker, layer as below:
Layer 1: 1/4 cup water
Layer 2: 2 cups sprouts (fenugreek/moong/chana)
Layer 3: 1/2 cup each (jaggery, sugar)
Layer 4: 1tsp amchur, 1/2tsp each (chilli powder, cumin powder, coriander powder, salt, garam masala powder), a pinch each (asafoetida, turmeric powder)

Cook on high for 2 whistles or 5 minutes. Release pressure. Mix in 1tbsp bottled tadka.

Thursday: Sour Fruit Launji

In a 2L Pressure Baker, layer as below.
Layer 1: 2tbsp oil
Layer 2: 2 cups chopped sour fruits (mango/tomato/sour grapes/pineapple)
Layer 3: 1 cup sugar
Layer 4: 1/2tsp each (chilli powder, salt), a pinch of turmeric powder

Cook on high for 2 whistles or 5 minutes. Release pressure. Mix in 1tbsp bottled tadka.

Friday: Dry Fruit Launji

Prep.: Soak 1.5 cups dry fruits (dates/raisins/figs) in water for 2 hours. Drain.

In a 2L Pressure Baker, layer as below.
Layer 1: 1/4 cup water
Layer 2: Dry fruits
Layer 3: 1/2 cup jaggery, 1tsp amchur
Layer 4: 1/2tsp each (chilli powder, salt), a pinch of turmeric powder

Cook on high for 2 whistles or 5 minutes. Release pressure. Mix in 1tbsp bottled tadka.

Saturday: Spice-based Launji

In a 2L Pressure Baker, layer as below:
Layer 1: 2tbsp oil
Layer 2: 1 cup chopped (ginger/garlic cloves/chilli)
Layer 3: 1/2 cup jaggery, 1tsp amchur
Layer 4: 1/2tsp each (chilli powder, salt), a pinch of turmeric powder

Cook on high for 2 whistles or 4 minutes. Release pressure. Mix in 1tbsp bottled tadka.

Sunday: Sun-dried Vegetable Launji

Prep.: Soak 1 cup sun-dried vegetables in buttermilk for 2 hours. Drain.

In a 2L Pressure Baker, layer as below:
Layer 1: 1/4 cup water
Layer 2: Soaked sun-dried vegetables
Layer 3: 1/2 cup jaggery, 1tsp amchur
Layer 4: 1/2tsp each (chilli powder, salt), a pinch of turmeric powder

Cook on high for 2 whistles or 5 minutes. Release pressure. Mix in 1tbsp bottled tadka.

Common tadka:

Fenugreek seeds, mustard seeds, fennel seeds, dry red chillies in oil.

Tip

Can sprinkle ginger powder over top layer.

KANNADIGA CHITRANNA* (SOUTH INDIAN TAVA PULAV)

Base: Cooked Rice/Millets/Cauliflower Rice
Flavouring: Bottled Tadka (p. 26), Herbs
Additives: Fruits, Vegetables, Thokku, Spiced Powder, Yogurt

Monday: Classic Chitranna

Mix 1 cup cooked and cooled rice with 1tbsp bottled tadka, a pinch of roasted turmeric powder, 1tsp lemon juice, 1/4tsp salt.

Tuesday: Vegetable-based Chitranna

In a 2L Pressure Baker, layer as below:
Layer 1: 1tbsp each (oil, water)
Layer 2: 2 cups finely chopped vegetables (cabbage, carrot)
Layer 3: 1/2tsp salt, 2 chopped green chillies

Cook on high for 2 whistles or 5 minutes. Release pressure. Mix with 1 cup cooked and cooled rice, 1tbsp bottled tadka.

Wednesday: Thokku/Gojju-based Chitranna

In a 2L Pressure Baker, layer as below:
Layer 1: 3tbsp oil
Layer 2: 4 chopped green chillies
Layer 3: 2 cups finely chopped (onion/garlic/brinjal, deseeded tomato/ ginger, etc.), or 4 cups chopped herbs (mint, curry leaves, etc.)
Layer 4: 1tbsp tamarind paste, 1/2tsp salt

Cook on high for 4 whistles or 5 minutes. Let pressure settle. Mash/ blend. Mix 1tbsp each (mashed paste, bottled tadka) with 1 cup cooked and cooled rice.

---

*   Meals with starch

Thursday: Spice Powder-based Chitranna

Mix 1 cup cooked and cooled rice with 1 tbsp each (spiced powder [pepper-cumin powder/puliyogare powder/sesame seed powder, etc.], bottled tadka).

Friday: Pickle-based Chitranna

Mix 1 cup cooked and cooled rice with 1 tbsp each (pickle, bottled tadka).

Saturday: Fruit-based Chitranna

In a 2L Pressure Baker, layer as below:
Layer 1: 1 tbsp each (water, oil)
Layer 2: 2 cups finely chopped mixed fruits (raw mango, pineapple, etc.)
Layer 3: 1/2tsp salt, 2 chopped green chillies

Cook on high for 2 whistles. Release pressure. Mix with 1 cup cooked and cooled rice, 1 tbsp bottled tadka.

Sunday: Yogurt-based Chitranna

Coarsely mash and mix 1 cup each (cooked and cooled rice, yogurt), 1 tbsp bottled tadka, 1/2tsp salt.

Common tadka:

Mustard seeds, dry red chillies, asafoetida, curry leaves, split urad dal, chana dal, green chillies, ginger, peanuts, cashewnut in oil.

MUGHLAI BIRYANI (RICE AND MEAT CASSEROLE)

Base: Rice, Vegetables, Chicken, Meat, Seafood
Flavouring: Caramelized Onion (p. 27), Spices, Ginger-garlic Paste (p. 28), Mint, Bottled Tadka (p. 26)
Additives: Fried Onion, Cilantro, Fried Nuts/Raisins

Monday: Kuska Biryani (Empty Biryani)

Prep.: Soak 2 cups basmati in water for 30 minutes. Drain. (2 cups basmati is 400g unsoaked or 550g [3.5 cups soaked].)

In a 2L Pressure Baker, add 1tbsp ghee, 3 cups water, 1/4 cup each (yogurt, chopped mint, caramelized onion), 1tsp each (biryani masala, salt), rice. Mix everything.

Cook on high for 2 whistles or 10 minutes. Let pressure settle. Fluff up.

Tuesday: Vegetable Biryani

Prep.: Soak 1 cup basmati rice in water for 30 minutes. Drain. Mix 4 cups chopped mushroom/4 cups soaked soya chunks/2 cups chopped raw jackfruit, 1/4 cup each (yogurt, chopped mint, caramelized onion), 1tsp each (biryani masala, chilli powder, salt), 1tbsp ginger-garlic paste, 2 slit green chillies.

In a 2L Pressure Baker, layer as below:
Layer 1: 1tbsp ghee, 1/4 cup water
Layer 2: Half the spiced mushroom/soya/jackfruit mixture
Layer 3: Rice
Layer 4: Remaining half of spiced mushroom/soya/jackfruit mixture to cover the rice completely

Cook on high for 4 whistles or 7minutes. Let pressure settle. Mix everything, fluff up and serve.

Wednesday: Qabooli Biryani (Dal Biryani)

Prep.: Soak 1 cup basmati rice in water for 30 minutes. Drain. Chana dal mixture: Soak 1/2 cup chana dal for 2 hours. Drain. Mix soaked chana dal, 1/2 cup whisked yogurt, 1/4 cup chopped mint, 3tbsp caramelized onions, 1tsp each (biryani masala, chilli powder, salt), 1tbsp ginger-garlic paste, 2 slit green chillies.

In a 2L Pressure Baker, layer as below:
Layer 1: 1 cup water, 1tbsp ghee
Layer 2: Rice
Layer 3: Cover with chana dal mixture

Cook on high for 4 whistles or 7 minutes. Let pressure settle. Mix everything. Fluff up and serve.

Thursday: Chicken Biryani

See p. 41 for recipe.

Friday: Fish Biryani

Prep.: Soak 1 cup basmati rice in water for 30 minutes. Drain. Mix 250g thick fish cubes, 2tbsp each caramelized (onion, tomato), 1/4 cup mint, 1tsp each (biryani masala, chilli powder, salt), 1tbsp ginger-garlic paste, 2 slit green chillies.

In a 2L Pressure Baker, layer as below:
Layer 1: 1 cup water, 1tbsp ghee
Layer 2: Rice
Layer 3: Cover with spiced fish

Cook on high for 2 whistles or 6 minutes. Let pressure settle. Remove fish. Mix and fluff up rice. Mix everything and serve.

Saturday: Prawn Biryani

Prep.: Soak 1 cup basmati rice in water for 30 minutes. Drain. Mix 400g big prawns, 2tbsp each caramelized (onion, tomato), 1/4 cup mint, 1tsp each (biryani masala, chilli powder, salt), 1tbsp ginger-garlic paste, 2 slit green chillies.

In a 2L Pressure Baker, add 1 cup water, 1tbsp ghee, rice, cover with spiced prawns.

Cook on high for 2 whistles or 6 minutes. Let pressure settle. Mix everything. Fluff up and serve.

Sunday: Mutton Biryani

Prep.: Soak 1 cup basmati rice in water for 30 minutes. Drain. Mix 500g tender (boneless) mutton chopped small, 1/2 cup yogurt, 1/4 cup chopped mint, 3tbsp caramelized onion, 1.5tsp each (biryani masala, chilli powder, salt), 1tbsp ginger-garlic paste, 2 slit green chillies.

In a 2L Pressure Baker, layer as below:
Layer 1: 1/2 cup water, 1tbsp ghee
Layer 2: 1/2 cup chopped tomato
Layer 3: Half the spiced meat (see prep.)
Layer 4: Rice
Layer 5: Cover with the remaining meat

Cook on high for 8 whistles or 10 minutes. Let pressure settle. Mix everything, fluff up and serve.

Common tadka:

Bay leaf, whole (cinnamon, cardamom, star anise, cloves) in ghee.

Garnish:

Fried onion, fried cashews/raisins, saffron strands soaked in milk, cilantro.

Tips

- Wash and rinse rice multiple times to remove starch.
- Soak the rice marinate meats longer if you face instances of them remaining undercooked.
- Can use any meat tenderizer like lemon/raw papaya paste in meat marinade.
- Can add more/less caramelized onion, ginger-garlic paste, spices, salt.
- Use small pieces of tender meat.
- Replace yogurt with coconut milk for a vegan version.
- Replace water with stock and add bottled tadka oil for greater flavour.
- Do not use vegetables like carrot/beans/cauliflower as they overcook. Instead, Pressure Bake and mix them into Kuska Biryani. Else use tough vegetables like potato.
- Can mix in paneer/boiled egg with Kuska Biryani for Paneer Biryani/Egg Biryani.
- Fluff up after the biryani cools a bit as rice grains are very delicate when hot.

MUGHLAI PULAV (FLAVOURED RICE)

Base: Rice
Flavouring: Herbs, Spices, Bottled Tadka (p. 26)
Additives: Fried Onion, Cilantro, Fried Nuts/Raisins

Monday: Vegetable-based Pulav #1

Prep.: Soak 2 cups basmati rice in water for 30 minutes. Drain. (2 cups basmati is 400g unsoaked or 550g [3.5 cups soaked].)

In a 2L Pressure Baker, add 1 tbsp ghee, 3 cups water, 1 bay leaf, 1 cup chopped hard vegetables (potato, raw jackfruit, carrot, sweet corn, beetroot, mushroom), 1tsp each (salt, ginger-garlic paste), 1/2tsp biryani masala, 2 slit chillies, rice. Mix everything. Cook on high for 2 whistles or 10 minutes. Let pressure settle. Fluff up.

Monday: Vegetable-based Pulav #2

Prep.: Crush, wash and drain 100g string hoppers (idiyappam).

In a 2L Pressure Baker, layer as below:
Layer 1: 1/4 cup water, 2tsp oil
Layer 2: 1/2 cup each (chopped [beans, carrot], fresh green peas)
Layer 3: 1tsp ginger-garlic paste, 1/2tsp salt, 1/4tsp turmeric powder, 1 chopped chilli
Layer 4: 1 cup idiyappam/string hoppers

Cook on high for 2 whistles or 4 minutes. Release pressure. Fluff up. Mix everything and serve.

Tuesday: Herb-based Pulav

Prep.: Soak 1 cup basmati rice in water for 30 minutes. Drain.

In a 2L Pressure Baker, add 2tbsp ghee, 1 cup water, 1 bay leaf, 2tbsp dry herbs (kasuri methi/rosemary/thyme) or 1/2 cup fresh herbs (mint, parsley, basil), 1tsp salt, 2 slit green chillies, rice.

Cook on high for 2 whistles or 7 minutes. Let pressure settle. Mix everything, fluff up and serve.

Wednesday: Sprouts-based Pulav

Prep.: Soak 1 cup basmati rice in water for 30 minutes. Drain.

In a 2L Pressure Baker, add 2tbsp ghee, 1 bay leaf, 1 cup each (water, sprouts [moong, masoor, chana, horse gram], 1tsp each (salt, ginger-garlic paste), 1/2tsp biryani masala, 2 slit green chillies, rice.

Cook on high for 2 whistles or 7 minutes. Let pressure settle. Mix everything, fluff up and serve.

Thursday: Fruit-based Pulav

Prep.: Soak 1 cup basmati rice in water for 30 minutes. Drain.

In a 2L Pressure Baker, add 2tbsp ghee, 1 cup water, 1 bay leaf, 1 cup each (water, chopped fruits [pineapple, tomato, mango]), 1tsp each (salt, ginger-garlic paste), 1/2tsp biryani masala, 2 slit green chillies, rice.

Cook on high for 2 whistles or 7 minutes. Let pressure settle. Mix everything, fluff up and serve.

Friday: Nut/Dry fruit-based Pulav

Prep.: Soak 1 cup basmati rice in water for 30 minutes. Drain.

In a 2L Pressure Baker, add 2tbsp ghee, 1 cup water, 1 bay leaf, 1/2 cup nuts (soaked almonds, cashew, walnut), 1/4 cup dry fruits (raisins, figs), 1tsp each (salt, ginger-garlic paste), 1/2tsp biryani masala, 2 slit chillies, rice.

Cook on high for 2 whistles or 7 minutes. Let pressure settle. Mix everything, fluff up and serve.

Saturday: Spice-based Pulav

Prep.: Soak 1 cup basmati rice in water for 30 minutes. Drain.

In a 2L Pressure Baker, add 2tbsp ghee, 1 cup water, 1 bay leaf, 2tbsp ginger paste/garlic paste/1tbsp roasted cumin, 1tsp salt, 1/2tsp biryani masala, 2 slit green chillies, rice.

Cook on high for 2 whistles or 7 minutes. Let pressure settle. Mix everything, fluff up and serve.

Sunday: Zarda Pulav

Prep.: Soak 1 cup basmati rice in water for 30 minutes. Drain.

In a 2L Pressure Baker, add 2tbsp ghee, 1 cup water, 1 bay leaf, 2 crushed cardamom, 1 inch cinnamon, rice.

Cook on high for 2 whistles or 7 minutes. Let pressure settle. Mix in 1/2 cup powdered sugar/jaggery, 10 saffron strands, fried (nuts, raisins). Let rest for 10 minutes.

Common tadka:

Bay leaf, whole (cinnamon, cardamom, star anise, cloves) in ghee.

Garnish:

Fried onion, fried cashews/raisins, saffron strands soaked in milk, cilantro

Tips

- Wash and rinse rice multiple times to remove starch.
- Soak the rice longer if you think it may remain undercooked.
- Replace a part of water with milk/coconut milk.
- Replace water with stock for greater flavour.
- Can mix in paneer after cooking.
- Fluff up after pulav cools a bit as rice grains are very delicate when hot.
- Can use soaked soya chunks/whey water for a protein punch.

TAVA PULAV

Base: Starch, Onion-Tomato
Flavouring: Ginger-garlic Paste (p. 28), Spices
Additives: Grain Flakes, Grated Cheese, Bhujia/Sev

Monday: Classic Tava Pulav

In a 2L Pressure Baker, layer as below:
Layer 1: 1tbsp each (oil, butter)
Layer 2: 1/2 cup each chopped (onion, tomato) in bull's-eye method
Layer 3: 1/2 cup each chopped (carrot, beans)
Layer 4: 1tsp ginger-garlic paste, 1/2tsp each (chilli powder, salt, pav bhaji masala), PIP – 1/4 cup peas

Cook on high for 2 whistles or 4 minutes. Release pressure. Mix in 1 cup cooked rice. Fluff up and keep closed for 5 minutes.

Tuesday: Oats/Poha/Roti Tava Pulav

In a 2L Pressure Baker, layer as below:
Layer 1: 1tbsp each (oil, butter)
Layer 2: 1/2 cup each chopped (onion, tomato) arranged in bull's-eye method
Layer 3: 1/2 cup each chopped (carrot, beans)
Layer 4: 1tsp ginger-garlic paste, 1/2tsp each (chilli powder, salt, pav bhaji masala), PIP – 1/4 cup peas

Cook on high for 2 whistles or 4 minutes. Release pressure. Mix in 1 cup quick-cooking oats/pressed rice/chopped flatbreads. Fluff up and keep closed for 5 minutes.

Wednesday: Rava Palak Pulav

In a 2L Pressure Baker, layer as below:
Layer 1: 1tbsp each (oil, butter)
Layer 2: 1/2 cup each chopped (onion, tomato) arranged in bull's-eye method.

Layer 3: 1/2 cup each chopped (carrot, beans)
Layer 4: 1/2 cup double-roasted rava mixed with 1 cup chopped spinach
Layer 5: 1tsp ginger-garlic paste, 1/2tsp each (chilli powder, salt, pav bhaji masala), PIP – 1/4 cup peas

Cook on high for 2 whistles or 4 minutes. Release pressure. Mix everything and fluff up.

Thursday: Kheema Tava Pulav

In a 2L Pressure Baker, layer as below:
Layer 1: 1tbsp each (oil, butter)
Layer 2: 1 cup minced meat spread to cover base
Layer 3: 1tsp ginger-garlic paste, 1/2tsp each (chilli powder, salt, garam masala powder)

Cook on high for 5 whistles or 6 minutes. Release pressure. Mash mince to separate into flakes. Mix in 1 cup cooked rice.

Friday: Paneer Tava Pulav

In a 2L Pressure Baker, layer as below:
Layer 1: 1tbsp each (oil, butter)
Layer 2: 1/2 cup each chopped (onion, tomato) arranged in bull's-eye method
Layer 3: 1/2 cup each chopped (carrot, beans)
Layer 4: PIP – 1/4 cup (paneer, peas), 1tsp ginger-garlic paste, 1/2tsp each (chilli powder, salt, pav bhaji masala)

Cook on high for 2 whistles or 4 minutes. Release pressure. Mix in 1 cup cooked rice. Fluff up and keep closed for 5 minutes.

Saturday: Paleo Tava Pulav

In a 2L Pressure Baker, layer as below:
Layer 1: 3tbsp ghee
Layer 2: 1/2 cup each chopped (onion, tomato) arranged in bull's-eye method.

Layer 3: PIP – 2 cups grated cauliflower mixed with 1tsp ginger-garlic paste, 1/2tsp each (chilli powder, salt, pav bhaji masala)

Cook on high for 3 whistles or 4 minutes. Release pressure. Mix everything.

Sunday: Schezwan Tava Pulav

In a 2L Pressure Baker, layer as below:
Layer 1: 1tbsp each (oil, butter)
Layer 2: 1/4 cup each chopped (onion, spring onion), 1 chopped garlic clove
Layer 3: 1/2 cup each chopped (carrot, beans)
Layer 4: PIP – 1/4 cup peas, 1tbsp Schezwan sauce, 1/2tsp salt

Cook on high for 2 whistles or 4 minutes. Release pressure. Mix in 1 cup cooked rice.

SOUTH INDIAN UPMA (SPICED GRITS)

Base: Processed Grain
Flavouring: Herbs, Spices
Additives: Vegetables, Roasted Nuts, Coconut

Monday: Rava Upma

In a 2L Pressure Baker, add 2 cups water, 1tsp salt, 2 chopped green chillies, 5 curry leaves, 1tbsp chopped ginger.

Cook on high for 1 whistle or 5 minutes. Release pressure. Mix in 1/2 cup double-roasted rava, 1tsp bottled tadka.
Close and rest for 15 minutes.

Tuesday: Aval Upma

Prep.: Wash and drain 1 cup poha.

In a 2L Pressure Baker, layer as below:
Layer 1: 2tbsp oil
Layer 2: 1/2 cup each chopped (onion, tomato)
Layer 3: 2 chopped green chillies, 1/2tsp salt, 1/4tsp turmeric powder

Cook on high for 4 whistles or 5 minutes. Release pressure. Mix in poha, 1tsp bottled tadka, 1/4 cup grated coconut.

Wednesday: Bread and Egg Upma

In a 2L Pressure Baker, layer as below:
Layer 1: 2tbsp oil
Layer 2: 1/2 cup each chopped (onion, tomato)
Layer 3: 2 chopped green chillies, 1/2tsp salt, 1/4tsp turmeric powder
Layer 4: 2 well-washed eggs

Cook on high for 4 whistles or 5 minutes. Release pressure. Let eggs cool and chop. Mix in 2 cups chopped bread/chopped roti, 1tsp each (pepper, bottled tadka).

Thursday: Semiya Upma

In a 2L Pressure Baker, add 1tsp oil, 1 cup roasted vermicelli and 1 cup water, 1/2tsp salt, 2 chopped green chillies, 5 curry leaves, 1tbsp chopped ginger. Cook on high for 1 whistle or 6 minutes. Let pressure settle.

Friday: Oats Upma

In a 2L Pressure Baker, layer as below:
Layer 1: 1/4 cup water
Layer 2: 2 cups chopped mixed vegetables
Layer 3: 2 chopped green chillies, 1tsp ginger-garlic paste, 1/2tsp salt, 1/4tsp turmeric powder

Cook on high for 2 whistles or 5 minutes. Release pressure. Mix in 1 cup quick-cooking oats, 1tsp bottled tadka.

Saturday: Borugula Upma

Prep.: Wash 2 cups puffed rice in water and drain.

In a 2L Pressure Baker, layer as below:
Layer 1: 1tbsp oil
Layer 2: 1/2 cup each chopped (onion, tomato)
Layer 3: 2 chopped green chillies, 1/2tsp salt, 1/4tsp turmeric powder

Cook on high for 3 whistles or 5 minutes. Release pressure. Mix in puffed rice, 1tsp bottled tadka.

Sunday: Pasta Upma

In a 2L Pressure Baker, add 1tsp oil, 1 cup each (Indian macaroni, water), 1/2tsp salt, a pinch of turmeric powder, 1 chopped green chilli.

Cook on high for 2 whistles or 4 minutes. Release pressure. Mix everything. Keep closed for 5 minutes. Mix in 1tsp bottled tadka.

Common tadka:

Mustard seeds, curry leaves, dry red chillies in oil.

Tips

- Garnish with chopped cilantro.
- Can mix in roasted/fried nuts.
- Add yogurt to stretch the dish further.

MEXICAN BURRITO BOWL

Base: Vegetables, Meats, Beans
Flavouring: Spices, Sauces, Herbs
Additives: Sweet Corn, Rice, Cooked Grains, Corn Chips, Cheese

Monday: Vegetable Burrito Bowl

In a 2L Pressure Baker, layer as below:
Layer 1: 2tbsp oil
Layer 2: 1 cup onion petals cut to bite size, 2 crushed and chopped garlic cloves
Layer 3: 2 cups capsicum cut to bite size
Layer 4: 1/2 cup sweet corn
Layer 5: 1/2tsp each (crushed cumin, salt, oregano), 1tsp chilli flakes

Cook on high for 2 whistles or 4 minutes. Release pressure. Mix everything with 1/2 cup canned beans, 2tbsp each (salsa, sour cream, guacamole).

Tuesday: Meat Burrito Bowl

In a 2L Pressure Baker, layer as below:
Layer 1: 2tbsp oil
Layer 2: 2 crushed and chopped garlic cloves
Layer 3: 1 cup ground meat
Layer 4: 1/2tsp each crushed (cumin seeds, salt, oregano), 1tsp chilli flakes

Cook on high for 5 whistles or 6 minutes. Let pressure settle. Mix in 1/2 cup each chopped (onion, tomato, capsicum), 2tbsp guacamole, 1tbsp hung yogurt.

Wednesday: Breakfast Burrito Bowl

In a 2L Pressure Baker, layer as below:
Layer 1: 2tbsp oil
Layer 2: 1 cup onion petals cut to bite size, 2 crushed and chopped garlic cloves
Layer 3: 2 cups capsicum cut to bite size
Layer 4: 1/2 cup sweet corn
Layer 5: 1/2tsp each (crushed cumin seeds, salt, oregano), 1tsp chilli flakes
Layer 6: 2 well-washed eggs

Cook on high for 2 whistles or 4 minutes. Release pressure. Let eggs cool and chop. Mix everything with 1/4 cup grated cheese, 1tbsp each (pico de gallo, guacamole).

Thursday: Sprouts Burrito Bowl

In a 2L Pressure Baker, layer as below:
Layer 1: 2tbsp oil
Layer 2: 1 cup onion petals cut to bite size, 2 crushed and chopped garlic cloves
Layer 3: 2 cups sprouts
Layer 4: 1/2 cup sweet corn
Layer 5: 1/2tsp each (crushed cumin seeds, salt, crushed oregano), 1tsp chilli flakes
Layer 6: PIP – add 1 cup bite-sized capsicum

Cook on high for 2 whistles or 4 minutes. Mix everything with 1/4 cup each chopped (onion, tomato), 1 cup lettuce, 1tsp lemon juice.

Friday: Chicken Burrito Bowl (Meat, Cheese, Salsa)

In a 2L Pressure Baker, layer as below:
Layer 1: 2tbsp oil
Layer 2: 2 crushed and chopped garlic cloves

Layer 3: 1 cup boneless chicken chopped small
Layer 4: 1/2tsp each (crushed cumin seeds, salt, oregano), 1tsp chilli flakes
Layer 5: PIP – 1 cup cauliflower chopped big

Cook on high for 4 whistles or 5 minutes. Release pressure. Mix everything with 1/2 cup each chopped (onion, tomato, capsicum), 2tbsp salsa, 1tbsp hung yogurt.

Saturday: Fish Burrito Bowl

Layer 1: 2tbsp oil
Layer 2: 2 crushed and chopped garlic cloves
Layer 3: 250g boneless fish cubes cut big
Layer 4: 1/2tsp each (crushed cumin seeds, salt, crushed oregano), 1tsp chilli flakes

Cook on high for 3 whistles or 4 minutes. Release pressure. Mix in 1/2 cup each chopped (cabbage, onion, tomato), 2tbsp salsa, 1tsp lemon juice.

Sunday: Cheese and Chilli Burrito Bowl

Mix 1 cup chopped paneer, 1/4 cup each (chopped [feta, cheddar, mozzarella], crushed nachos), 1tsp each (olive oil, lemon juice), 1tbsp each (guacamole, roja), 2 cups torn lettuce, 1/2 cup each finely chopped (onion, tomato), 2 finely chopped green chillies, 1/4 cup crushed nachos.

Pico de gallo:

Mix 1/2 cup each finely chopped (tomato, onion), 2 finely chopped green chillies, 1tsp lemon juice, 1/4 cup finely chopped cilantro, 1/4tsp salt.

Guacamole:

Take 1 cup ripe avocado, 1/4tsp salt, 1 finely chopped green chilli, 1/4 cup finely chopped cilantro, 1tsp lemon juice. Mash everything together.

Salsa Roja:

In a 2L Pressure Baker, layer as below
Layer 1: 2tbsp oil
Layer 2: 1/4 cup chopped onion, 2 cups chopped tomato, 2 chopped green chillies, 1/2tsp salt

Cook on high for 7 minutes. Let pressure settle. Mash everything. Mix in 1tbsp chopped cilantro.

Tips

- Can add cooked rice/millets/quinoa, corn chips.
- Can roll into a flatbread as a burrito.
- Can mix in cold cuts.
- Can mix in any salad dressing.
- Can serve in hollowed-out fruits/vegetables.

GUJARATI DHOKLA (STEAMED BATTER CAKES)

Base: Dals, Grains
Flavouring: Ginger, Garlic, Chillies, Bottled Tadka (p. 26)
Additives: Vegetables, Herbs

Monday: Khaman Dhokla (Gram Flour-based Dhokla)

Mix 1 cup besan, 2tbsp rava, 1tsp each (sugar, ginger-garlic paste, lemon juice, green chilli paste), 1/2tsp salt, 2tsp oil, 3/4 cup water. Let it rest for 10 minutes. Mix in 1tsp fruit salt, 2tsp water till batter gets frothy.

Tuesday: Dal–Rice Flour-based Dhokla

Mix 1.5 cup dhokla flour, 1/2 cup each (sour yogurt, water), 1tsp each (ginger-garlic paste, green chilli paste, crushed black pepper corns, salt), 2tsp oil. Let it ferment for 5 to 6 hours. Mix in 1tsp fruit salt,

2tsp water till batter gets frothy. Can use any grain/lentil flour or any combination of them.

Wednesday: Dal–Rice Batter-based Dhokla

Take 2 cups ready-made idli batter. Mix in 1tsp each (ginger-garlic paste, green chilli paste, crushed black pepper corns, salt), 2tsp oil. Mix in 1tsp fruit salt, 2tsp water till batter gets frothy. Can use any grain/lentil batter or any combination of them.

Thursday: Grain Grits-based Dhokla (Rava Dhokla)

Mix 1 cup rava, 1/4 cup sour yogurt, 1 cup water, 1tsp each (ginger-garlic paste, green chilli paste, salt), 2tsp oil. Let it rest for 10 minutes. Mix in 1tsp fruit salt, 2tsp water till batter gets frothy.

Friday: Vegetable Dhokla

Mix 1 cup rava, 1/4 cup each (grated carrot, green peas), 1/2 cup each (sour yogurt, water), 1tsp each (ginger-garlic paste, green chilli paste, salt), 2tsp oil. Let it rest for 10 minutes. Mix in 1tsp fruit salt, 2tsp water till batter gets frothy.

Saturday: Palak Dhokla

Mix 1 cup besan, 1/4 cup rava, 1 cup chopped spinach, 1tsp each (salt, sugar, green chilli paste, ginger-garlic paste), 2tsp oil, 1/4tsp citric acid dissolved in 1tbsp water. Let it rest for 10 minutes. Mix in 1tsp fruit salt, 2tsp water till batter gets frothy.

Sunday: Oats Rava Dhokla (Mixed Grains Dhokla)

Mix 1/2 cup each (quick-cooking oats, rava, yogurt, water), 1tsp each (ginger-garlic paste, green chilli paste), 1/2tsp salt, 2tsp oil. Let rest for 10 minutes. Mix in 1tsp fruit salt, 2tsp water till batter gets frothy.

Cooking Instructions:

In 2L/3L/4.5L Pressure Baker, add 1 cup water. Place a greased inner wide bowl with batter. Cook on high for 6 whistles. Let pressure settle. Unmould and slice into squares. Add bottled tadka, garnish.

Common tadka:

Mustard seeds, sesame seeds, curry leaves in oil.

Garnish:

Cilantro, grated coconut

Dhokla styles

a. Mini Dhoklas:
   Pour batter in mini idli moulds and cook on high for 3 whistles.

b. Idli Dhoklas:
   Pour batter in shallow idli moulds/thatte idli moulds and cook on high for 3 whistles.

c. Rasila Dhokla:
   Mix 1tbsp sugar, 1/2 cup hot water. Pour over cooked dhoklas.

d. Sandwich Dhokla:
   Pour alternating layers of dhokla batter in mould and steam together.

e. Idada Dhokla (flat, non-fermented, non-leavened dhokla):
   Use any batter above and cook it as above without fermentation.

Tips

- Make sure batter is of the consistency of dosa batter.
- If batter is too thick, add water. If too thin, add flour.
- The batter should resemble a foam for fluffy dhoklas.
- The South Indian idli/rava idli are dhokla variants.

GUJARATI MUTHIYA (STEAMED DUMPLINGS)

Base: Grits/Flours
Flavouring: Spices, Bottled Tadka (p. 26)
Additives: Vegetables, Herbs

Monday: Classic Muthiyas

Mix 1 cup gram flour, 1/4 cup wholewheat flour, 1tbsp rava, 1/2 cup yogurt, 2 finely chopped green chillies, 1tsp each (kasuri methi, grated ginger, oil), 1/2tsp each (salt, cumin, coriander powder), a pinch each (asafoetida, turmeric powder). Let rest for 10 minutes. Knead to a dough.

Tuesday: Vegetable-based Muthiyas

Mix 1 cup gram flour, 1/4 cup whole wheat flour, 1tbsp rava, 1 cup grated bottle gourd or any watery vegetables (zucchini, Malabar cucumber, white pumpkin), 2 finely chopped green chillies, 1tsp each (kasuri methi, grated ginger, oil), 1/2tsp each (salt, cumin, coriander powder), a pinch each (asafoetida, turmeric powder) Let rest for 10 minutes. Knead to a dough.

Wednesday: Edible Greens-based Muthiyas

Mix 1 cup gram flour, 2tbsp rava, 2 cups finely chopped fenugreek leaves or any spinach variety, 1/4 cup yogurt, 2 finely chopped green chillies, 1tsp each (kasuri methi, grated ginger, oil), 1/2tsp each (salt, cumin, coriander powder), a pinch each (asafoetida, turmeric powder). Let rest for 10 minutes.

Thursday: Herb-based Muthiyas

Mix 1 cup each (gram flour, finely chopped mint, finely chopped cilantro), 2tbsp rava, 1/4 cup yogurt, 2 finely chopped green chillies, 1tsp each (kasuri methi, grated ginger, oil), 1/2tsp each (salt, cumin, coriander powder), a pinch each (asafoetida, turmeric powder). Let rest for 10 minutes.

Friday: Mixed Flour and Mixed Veg-based Muthiyas

Take 1/4 cup each (gram flour, rava, soya flour, millet flour). Mix in 1/2 cup finely chopped spinach, 1/4 cup each (grated [cabbage, carrot], caramelized/fried onion, yogurt), 2 finely chopped green chillies, 1tsp each (kasuri methi, grated ginger), 1/4 cup oil, 1/2tsp each (salt, cumin), a pinch each (asafoetida, turmeric powder). Let rest for 10 minutes.

Saturday: Cooked Grain-based Muthiyas

Mix 1 cup cooked rice/rava upma, 1/4 cup gram flour, 1tbsp each finely chopped (green chillies, cilantro), 1tsp each (grated ginger, oil), 1/2tsp salt, a pinch of asafoetida, 2tbsp yogurt. Mash and mix into a dough.

Sunday: Cooked Grain and Lentil-based Muthiyas

Mix 1 cup cooked and mashed khichdi, 1/4 cup gram flour, 1tbsp each finely chopped (green chillies, cilantro), 1tsp each (grated ginger, oil), 1/2tsp salt, a pinch of asafoetida. Mash and mix into a dough.

Cooking instructions:

Knead to a dough. Shape into thin sausages or small balls with your fist (mutthi). Place in a wide inner bowl. In a 2L Pressure Baker, add 1 cup water. Place inner vessel with dumplings. Cook on high for 7 minutes. Let pressure settle. Mix with 1tbsp bottled tadka.

Common tadka:

Mustard seeds, cumin seeds, curry leaves, dry red chillies in oil.

Garnish:

Roasted sesame seeds, cilantro

Tips

- After cooking, check if a knife inserted comes out clean.
- Can slice into discs.
- Can mix in tadka.

- Can mix in 1/2tsp baking powder while kneading for a softer texture.
- Can use roasted gram flour.
- Add more gram flour if dough is too loose and more yogurt if too tight.

TAMIL PIDI KOZHUKATTAI (SOUTH INDIAN STEAMED DUMPLINGS/MUTHIYAS)

Base: Dals, Grains
Flavouring: Herbs, Spices, Bottled Tadka (p. 26)
Additives: Coconut, Jaggery

Monday: Ulundhu Kozhukattai (Dal-based)

Soak 1/2 cup split urad dal for 2 hours. Drain. Blend to a coarse paste with 3 green chillies, 1/2tsp salt, 1/4tsp asafoetida, 1tsp oil. Mix in 1tbsp bottled tadka. Shape into small balls.

Tuesday: Mixed Dal Kozhukattai (Mixed Dal-based)

Soak 1/4 cup each dal (tuvar, chana) for 2 hours. Drain. Blend to a coarse paste with 2 dry red chillies, 5 curry leaves, 1/2tsp salt, 1/4tsp asafoetida, 1tsp oil. Shape into small balls.

Wednesday: Aval Kozhukattai (Pressed Grain-based)

Blend 1 cup poha, 1/2 cup each (jaggery, coconut), 1/4tsp cardamom powder. Shape into small balls. Sprinkle water if needed.

Thursday: Rava Kozhukattai (Grain Grits-based)

Mix 1/2 cup double-roasted rava, 1/4 cup each (grated carrot, grated coconut, yogurt), 1 chopped green chilli, 1tbsp each (bottled tadka, chopped cashew), 1/2tsp each (salt, grated ginger). Shape into small balls.

Friday: No-cook Sweet Kozhukattai (Grain Flour-based)

Soak 1 cup raw rice for 1 hour. Drain. Spread out and let dry. Blend to a powder. Mix in 1 cup grated jaggery, 2tbsp ghee, a pinch each (salt, cardamom powder). Mix and knead to a dough. Pinch off small balls and shape into rounds. No cooking needed.

Saturday: Masala Kozhukattai (Dal and Spice-based)

Soak 1/4tsp each dal (moong, masoor) for 2 hours. Drain. Blend to a coarse paste with 2 dry red chillies, 1/4 cup chopped coconut, 1tsp ginger-garlic paste, 1/2tsp each (fennel, salt, garam masala powder), 1tsp oil, 5 curry leaves. Shape into small balls.

Sunday: Arisi Paruppu Kozhukattai (Dal and Grain-based)

Soak 1/4tsp each (chana dal, masoor dal, raw rice/millet) for 2 hours. Drain. Blend to a coarse paste with 2 dry red chillies, 5 curry leaves, 1/2tsp salt, 1/4tsp asafoetida, 1tsp oil. Shape into small balls.

Cooking instructions:

In a 2L Pressure Baker, add 1 cup water. Place the balls in a small inner vessel. Cook on high for 6 whistles or 7 minutes. Let pressure settle.

Tips

- Do not shape balls too hard or too large.
- After cooking, check if a knife inserted comes out clean.
- Can serve as a snack/stir-fry or simmer in curries as vegetable substitutes.

NORTH INDIAN MASALA (CARAMELIZED ONION–TOMATO STEW)

Base: Caramelized Onion/Tomato (p. 29)
Flavouring: Ginger-garlic Paste (p. 28), Garam Masala Powder
Additives: Vegetables, Legumes Meat/Egg/Seafood, Cream, Butter, Nut Paste, Stock (p. 53-54)

Monday: Classic Masala Base

In a 2L Pressure Baker, layer as below:
Layer 1: 3tbsp oil
Layer 2: 1 cup chopped onion, 4 small whole tomato
Layer 3: 1tbsp ginger-garlic paste, 1/2tsp each (salt, garam masala powder), 1tsp Kashmiri chilli powder

Cook on high for 4 whistles or 5 minutes. Release pressure. Mash and mix everything.

Tip

If using a big tomato, scoop out the seeds.

Tuesday: Mix Veg Masala

In a 2L Pressure Baker, layer as below:
Layer 1: 1/4 cup water
Layer 2: 1/2 cup each chopped (beans, carrot, baby corn)
Layer 3: 1 chopped green chilli, 1tsp ginger-garlic paste, 1/2tsp each (salt, garam masala powder)
Layer 4: PIP – 1/2 cup Classic Masala Base (above), 1/2 cup green peas

Cook on high for 3 whistles or 5 minutes. Release pressure. Mix everything with 1tbsp bottled tadka.

Wednesday: Chana Masala

Prep.: Soak 1/2 cup chickpeas overnight in water with 1/2tsp salt. Drain.

In a 2L Pressure Baker, layer as below:
Layer 1: 2tbsp oil
Layer 2: 1/2 cup each chopped (onion, tomato) in bull's-eye method
Layer 3: Chickpeas
Layer 4: 1 chopped green chilli, 1tsp ginger-garlic paste
Layer 5: 1/2tsp each (salt, chilli powder, garam masala powder)

Cook on high for 7 minutes. Let pressure settle. Coarsely mash. Mix everything.

Thursday: Chicken Masala

Prep.: Mix 250g chopped chicken with 1/2tsp each (salt, garam masala powder), 1/4tsp turmeric powder, 1tbsp ginger-garlic paste, 2 chopped green chillies.

In a 2L Pressure Baker, layer as below:
Layer 1: 2tbsp oil
Layer 2: Chopped chicken
Layer 3: PIP – 1/2 cup Classic Masala Base (p. 175)

Cook on high for 5 whistles or 6 minutes. Let pressure settle. Mix everything.

Friday: Egg Masala

In a 2L Pressure Baker, layer as below:
Layer 1: 2tbsp oil
Layer 2: 1/2 cup chopped onion and 1 cup chopped tomato in bull's-eye method
Layer 3: 1 chopped green chilli, 1tsp ginger-garlic paste
Layer 4: 1/2tsp each (salt, chilli powder, garam masala powder, pepper powder)
Layer 5: 4 well-washed eggs

Cook on high for 4 whistles or 5 minutes. Let pressure settle. Remove, peel and halve eggs. Coarsely mash gravy. Mix everything.

Saturday: Gobhi Masala

Prep.: Mix 250g cauliflower with 1/2tsp each (salt, garam masala powder), 1/4tsp turmeric powder, 1tbsp ginger-garlic paste, 2 chopped green chillies.

In a 2L Pressure Baker, layer as below:
Layer 1: 2tbsp oil
Layer 2: 1 cup chopped onion, 4 small whole tomato
Layer 3: PIP – spiced cauliflower (see prep.)

Cook on high for 4 whistles or 5 minutes. Release pressure. Remove inner vessel. Mash gravy. Mix everything.

Sunday: Poori Masala (South Indian No Onion–Tomato Masala)

In a 2L Pressure Baker, layer as below:
Layer 1: 1tsp oil, 1/4 cup water
Layer 2: 2 cups potato chopped small
Layer 3: 3 chopped green chillies, 5 crushed curry leaves, 1tbsp chopped ginger, 1/4tsp turmeric powder, 1/2tsp salt
Layer 4: PIP – 1/4 cup peas

Cook on high for 4 whistles or 5 minutes. Release pressure. Remove PIP. Mash coarsely with 1/2 cup water. Mix in peas and 1tbsp bottled tadka.

Accompaniments Module

NORTH INDIAN RAITA (YOGURT DIP)

Base: Yogurt
Flavouring: Spices, Herbs, Bottled Tadka (p. 26)
Additives: Vegetables, Fruits, Herbs, Vegetable Substitutes

Monday: Classic Raita

Mix 1 cup chopped/grated salad vegetables (cucumber/carrot/onion/ radish/tomato) with 1 cup yogurt, 1/4tsp salt.

Tuesday: Cooked/Mashed Veg Raita

In a 2L Pressure Baker, layer as below:
Layer 1: 1/4 cup water
Layer 2: 2 cups chopped vegetables
Layer 3: 1/4tsp salt

Cook on high for 2 whistles or 5 minutes. Release pressure. Let cool. Mix in 1 cup whisked yogurt. Or mash vegetables coarsely and mix in yogurt.

Wednesday: Blended Raita

Blend 1 cup packed herbs (mint/cilantro) or 1tbsp chopped (garlic/ ginger), 1 green chilli, 5 cashews, 1/2tsp salt, 1/4 cup yogurt to a paste. Mix in 1 cup whisked yogurt.

Thursday: Vegetable Substitute-based Raita

Mix 1/4 cup boondi/bhujia/sev with 1 cup yogurt.

Friday: Spice-based Raita

Mix 1tbsp bottled tadka/pickle/with 1 cup yogurt.

Saturday: Roasted Lentil Powder Raita

Mix 3tbsp roasted (urad dal powder/gram flour/paruppu podi/idli podi) with 1 cup yogurt, 1tsp bottled tadka, 1/4tsp salt.

Sunday: Fruit Raita

Mix 1/2 cup fresh/dry fruits with 1 cup yogurt, 1tbsp chopped nuts.

Tips

- Can use hung yogurt.
- Can mix in spice powders (cumin, pepper, chaat masala).
- Can mix in finely chopped chillies/herbs.
- Can mix in tadka of your choice.

KONKANI TAMBLI (BLENDED RAITA/YOGURT DIP)

Base: Coconut, Yogurt/Tamarind/Kokum
Additives: Vegetables, Fruits, Herbs, Spices, Peels, Seeds
Flavouring: Bottled Tadka (p. 26)

Monday: Classic Tambli

Blend 1/4 cup chopped coconut, 1 green chilli, 1/2tsp salt, 1/4 cup yogurt to a paste. Mix in 1/2 cup whisked yogurt, 1tsp bottled tadka.

Tuesday: Raw Vegetable Tambli

Blend 1/4 cup each (chopped coconut, yogurt, salad vegetables [carrot/onion/tomato/cucumber]), 2 green chillies, 1/2tsp salt to a paste. Mix in 1/2 cup yogurt, 1tsp bottled tadka.

Wednesday: Herb-based Tambli

Blend 1/4 cup each (chopped coconut, yogurt, herbs [cilantro/mint/ curry leaves/Brahmi leaves/ajwain leaves/fenugreek leaves]), 2 green chillies, 1/2tsp salt to a paste. Mix in 1/2 cup whisked yogurt, 1tsp bottled tadka.

Thursday: Fruit-based Tambli

Blend 1/4 cup each (chopped coconut, chopped fruits [raw mango/ gooseberry/pineapple], yogurt), 2 dry red chillies, 1/2tsp salt to a paste. Mix in 1/2 cup whisked yogurt, 1tsp bottled tadka.

Friday: Peel/Flower/Seed-based Tambli

In a 2L Pressure Baker, layer as below:
Layer 1: 1/4 cup water
Layer 2: 1 cup peels (ridge gourd, pomegranate) or 1 cup flowers (drumstick, banana flower) or 1 cup chopped jackfruit seeds
Layer 3: 1tsp tamarind paste

Cook on high for 2 whistles or 5 minutes. Release pressure. Blend with 1/4 cup chopped coconut, 2 dry red chillies, 1tsp each (pepper, cumin), 1/2tsp salt, 1/2 cup water.

Saturday: Shunti Belluli/Menthi Tambli (Spice-based Tambli)

Blend 1/4 cup each (chopped coconut, yogurt) 1tbsp chopped (ginger/ garlic) or 1/4tsp roasted fenugreek seed powder, 2 green chillies, 1/2tsp salt, to a paste. Mix in 1/2 cup yogurt, 1tsp bottled tadka.

Sunday: Soppu Tambli (Edible Greens Tambli)

In a 2L Pressure Baker, layer as below:
Layer 1: 1/4 cup water
Layer 2: 3 cups chopped edible greens (Mangalore spinach, spinach)
Layer 3: 1tsp tamarind paste

Cook on high for 2 whistles or 4 minutes. Release pressure. Blend with 1/4 cup each (coconut, yogurt), 2 dry red chillies, 1tbsp pepper, 1tsp cumin, 1/2tsp salt, 1/4 cup yogurt. Mix in 1 cup whisked yogurt, 1tsp bottled tadka.

Common tadka:

Mustard seeds, dry red chillies, cumin seeds.

TAMIL THOGAYAL/THUVAYAL (SOUR AND SPICY DIPS)

Base: Vegetables, Coconut, Lentils, Spices, Herbs, Peels, Spinach
Flavouring: Chillies, Pepper, Asafoetida, Fenugreek, Oil
Additives: Jaggery, Spiced Lentil Powder (p. 31), Roasted Gram, Bottled Tadka (p. 26)

Monday: Classic Thogayal (Coconut-based Dip)

Blend 1/2 cup chopped coconut, 5 dry red chillies, 1tsp tamarind paste, 1/4tsp salt, 1tsp coconut oil, 1/4 cup water to a coarse paste.

Tuesday: Paruppu/Pathiya Thogayal (Roasted Dal-based Dip)

Blend 1/2 cup dal/seeds (tuvar, chana, moong, masoor, horse gram, sesame, peanut), 1tbsp pepper, 1tsp oil, 1/2tsp salt, 1/2 cup water to a thick paste.

Wednesday: Vegetable-based Thogayal

In a 2L Pressure Baker, layer as below:
Layer 1: 2tbsp oil, 1tbsp water
Layer 2: 2 cups chopped non-watery vegetables (squash, carrot, cabbage, beetroot, ivy gourd, brinjal, banana flower, tender-bone vine, radish)
Layer 3: 3 dry red chillies, 1tsp tamarind paste
Layer 4: 2tbsp roasted lentil powder (paruppu podi)
Layer 5: 1/2tsp salt

Cook on high for 2 whistles or 4 minutes. Release pressure. Blend everything with 1tsp oil.

Thursday: Spice-based Thogayal

In a 2L Pressure Baker, layer as below:
Layer 1: 2tbsp oil, 1tbsp water
Layer 2: 1 cup garlic cloves/chopped ginger/shallots
Layer 3: 3 dry red chillies, 1tsp tamarind paste
Layer 4: 1/2tsp salt

Cook on high for 2 whistles or 4 minutes. Release pressure. Blend everything with 1tsp oil.

Friday: Peel-based Thogayal

In a 2L Pressure Baker, layer as below:
Layer 1: 2tbsp oil, 1tbsp water
Layer 2: 2 cups chopped ridge gourd peel/1 cup chopped orange peel
Layer 3: 3 dry red chillies, 1tsp tamarind paste
Layer 4: 2tbsp roasted lentil powder (paruppu podi)
Layer 5: 1/2tsp salt

Cook on high for 2 whistles or 4 minutes. Release pressure. Blend everything with 1tsp oil.

Saturday: Herb-based Thogayal

In a 2L Pressure Baker, layer as below:
Layer 1: 1/4 cup water
Layer 2: 4 cups packed herbs (curry leaves, mint, cilantro, fenugreek leaves)
Layer 3: 3 dry red chillies, 1tsp tamarind paste
Layer 4: 2tbsp roasted lentil powder (paruppu podi)
Layer 5: 1/2tsp salt

Cook on high for 2 whistles or 4 minutes. Release pressure. Blend everything with 1tsp oil.

Sunday: Keerai Thogayal (Green Dip)

In a 2L Pressure Baker, layer as below:

Layer 1: 1/4 cup water

Layer 2: 4 cups packed chopped greens (vallarai, manathakkali, agathi, murunga keerai, karisalankanni, pasalai, mudakathan, thoothuvalai)

Layer 3: 3 dry red chillies, 1tsp tamarind paste

Layer 4: 2tbsp roasted lentil powder (paruppu podi)

Layer 5: 1/2tsp salt

Cook on high for 2 whistles or 4 minutes. Release pressure. Blend everything with 1tsp oil.

Tips

- Can blend in garlic, caramelized onion, roasted fenugreek powder, asafoetida for flavour.
- Can blend in any variety of spiced lentil powder (paruppu podi)/ roasted gram/nuts for texture.
- Can increase tamarind/red chilli quantity and blend in jaggery to balance taste.
- Can mix in bottled tadka.
- Can blend in more oil to emulsify into a creamy dip.
- Layer over vegetables and Pressure Bake to make curries.
- Mix with rice to make variety rice.
- Serve with rice/rotis as a dip.

CHUTNEY (DIP)

Base: Vegetables, Coconut, Herbs, Nuts, Lentils
Flavouring: Bottled Tadka (p. 26)
Additives: Nuts/Roasted Lentils

Monday: Classic Coconut Chutney

Coconut + chillies + thickener (optional) + salt + oil = Coconut chutney

Blend 1/2 cup chopped coconut, 2 green chillies, 1/2tsp salt, 1tsp coconut oil, 1/4 cup water to a thick paste. Mix in 1tbsp bottled tadka.

Tuesday: Herb-based Chutney

Herbs + chillies + thickener + salt + oil = Herb chutney

Blend 4 cups of chopped mint/cilantro, 2 green chillies, 1/4 cup roasted peanuts, 1/2tsp salt, 1tsp oil, 1/4 cup water to a thick paste. Mix in 1tbsp bottled tadka.

Wednesday: Caramelized Chutneys (Ginger/Garlic, Shallots)

Caramelized vegetables + chillies + salt + oil = Caramelized chutney

In a 2L Pressure Baker, layer as below:
Layer 1: 3tbsp oil
Layer 2: 2 cups chopped (onion/shallots/ginger/garlic), 1 small whole tomato

Cook on high for 4 whistles or 5 minutes. Release pressure. Blend with 2 chopped green chillies, 1/2tsp salt. Mix in 1tbsp bottled tadka.

Thursday: Raw Vegetable-based Chutney

Salad vegetables + chillies + salt + oil = Raw vegetable chutney

Blend 1/4 cup chopped coconut, salad vegetables (carrot/onion/cucumber), 2 green chillies, 1/2tsp salt, 1tsp oil, 1/4 cup water to a thick paste. Mix in 1tbsp bottled tadka.

Friday: Nut-based Chutney

Nuts/lentils + chillies + salt + oil = Nut chutney

Blend 1/2 cup roasted (peanut/cashew/lentils), 3 green chillies, 1/2tsp salt, 1tsp oil, 1/4 cup water to a thick paste. Mix in 1tbsp bottled tadka.

Saturday: Fruit-based Chutney

Fruits + chillies + salt + oil = Fruit chutney

Blend 1/4 cup chopped coconut, 1/4 cup fruits (mango/pineapple/apple), 2 green chillies, 1/2tsp salt, 1tsp oil, 1/4 cup water to a thick paste. Mix in 1tbsp bottled tadka.

Sunday: Cooked Vegetable-based Chutney

Cooked vegetables + chillies + salt + oil = Cooked vegetable chutney

In a 2L Pressure Baker, layer as below:
Layer 1: 1/4 cup water, 2tbsp oil
Layer 2: 2 cups chopped vegetables

Cook on high for 2 whistles or 5 minutes. Release pressure. Blend with 2 chopped green chillies, 1/2tsp salt to a thick paste.

Tips

- Blending in coconut/nuts/roasted lentils thicken a chutney.
- Blending in oil emulsifies it.

TAMIL GOTHSU (SOUR VEGETABLE MASH)

Base: Vegetables/Fruits/Spinach
Flavouring: Bottled Tadka (p. 26), Ginger, Spice Powders, Herbs
Additives: Jaggery, Tamarind Pulp, Lemon Juice, Cooked Dal, Roasted Dal Powder, Coconut Paste, Gram Flour, Crushed Papad

Monday: Classic Brinjal Gothsu

In a 2L Pressure Baker, layer as below:
Layer 1: 3tbsp sesame oil
Layer 2: 1 chopped green chilli, 2 cups brinjal chopped small
Layer 3: 1tsp tamarind paste
Layer 4: 1/2tsp each (jaggery, salt), a pinch each (turmeric powder, asafoetida)

Cook on high for 3 whistles or 5 minutes. Release pressure. Mash everything with 1tbsp paruppu podi, 1/4 cup water. Mix in 2tsp bottled tadka.

Tuesday: Tomato Gothsu

In a 2L Pressure Baker, layer as below:
Layer 1: 2tbsp oil
Layer 2: 2 cups chopped deseeded tomato
Layer 3: 1/2 cup vegetables chopped small (potato, carrot)
Layer 4: 1/2tsp each (jaggery, salt)

Cook on high for 4 whistles or 6 minutes. Release pressure. Mash everything. Mix in 2tsp bottled tadka.

Wednesday: Pongal/Tiffin Gothsu

In a 2L Pressure Baker, layer as below:
Layer 1: 3tbsp oil
Layer 2: 2 chopped green chillies, 2 cups brinjal chopped small
Layer 3: 1/2 cup mixed vegetables chopped small (potato, carrot, squash), 1/4 cup cooked moong dal
Layer 4: 1tsp tamarind paste
Layer 5: 1/2tsp each (jaggery, salt), a pinch each (turmeric powder, asafoetida)

Cook on high for 3 whistles or 5 minutes. Release pressure. Mash everything with 1/4 cup water. Mix in 2tsp bottled tadka.

Thursday: Kalyana Gothsu (Mixed Gothsu)

In a 2L Pressure Baker, layer as below:
Layer 1: 2tbsp oil
Layer 2: 1/2 cup each chopped (onion, tomato)
Layer 3: 2 cups chopped mixed vegetables (potato, carrot, beans)
Layer 4: 1/4 cup cooked dal (tuvar, moong, chana, masoor)
Layer 5: 2tsp tamarind paste
Layer 6: 1tsp sambar powder, 1/2tsp each (jaggery, salt), a pinch each (turmeric powder, asafoetida)

Cook on high for 3 whistles or 6 minutes. Release pressure. Mash coarsely with 1/2 cup water. Mix in 2tsp bottled tadka.

Friday: Fruit Gothsu

In a 2L Pressure Baker, layer as below:
Layer 1: 2tbsp water
Layer 2: 1 chopped green chilli, 2 cups peeled and chopped fruits (mango, pineapple)
Layer 3: 1tbsp paruppu podi
Layer 4: 1/2tsp each (jaggery, salt), 1/4tsp turmeric powder

Cook on high for 3 whistles or 6 minutes. Release pressure. Mash everything with 1/4 cup water. Mix in 2tsp bottled tadka.

Saturday: Bitter Vegetable Gothsu

In a 2L Pressure Baker, layer as below:
Layer 1: 2tbsp oil
Layer 2: 2 cups bitter vegetables (chopped bitter gourd/Turkey berry) mixed with 1/2tsp each (salt, sambar powder)
Layer 3: PIP – mix 1 cup water with 1tbsp each (paruppu podi, thengai molagapodi, tamarind paste, jaggery)

Cook on high for 3 whistles or 6 minutes. Release pressure. Mix everything. Mix in 2tsp bottled tadka.

Sunday: Vegetable Gothsu

In a 2L Pressure Baker, layer as below:
Layer 1: 2tbsp oil
Layer 2: 1 chopped green chilli, 2 cups chopped country vegetables (ridge gourd, snake gourd)
Layer 3: 1/2tsp each (ginger-garlic paste, caramelized onion, jaggery, salt), 1 crushed papad

Cook on high for 2 whistles or 5 minutes. Release pressure. Mash coarsely. Mix in 1/4 cup water, 2tsp bottled tadka.

Making Paruppu podi:

Blend 1/4 cup roasted gram/lentils with 2 dry red chillies, 1/2tsp salt to a powder.

Making thengai molagapodi:

Blend 1/4 cup each (desiccated coconut, roasted gram/lentils), with 3 dry red chillies, 1/2tsp salt to a powder.

TAMIL MASIYAL/KADAYAL (DIP)

Base: Vegetables, Fruits, Spinach, Sprouts, Dal
Flavouring: Spices, Bottled Tadka (p. 26)
Additives: Lemon Juice, Ghee

Monday: Paruppu Masiyal

Prep.: Soak 1/4 cup dal (tuvar/moong/masoor/chana) in water for 2 hours. Drain.

In a 2L Pressure Baker, layer as below:
Layer 1: 1tbsp ghee, 1/4 cup water
Layer 2: Dal
Layer 3: 1/2tsp salt, a pinch each (asafoetida, turmeric powder), 1 slit green chilli

Cook on high for 4 whistles or 5 minutes. Let pressure settle. Mash. Mix in 1/2 cup water, 1 tbsp bottled tadka.

Tuesday: Keerai Masiyal

In a 2L Pressure Baker, layer as below:
Layer 1: 1/4 cup water
Layer 2: 4 cups finely chopped spinach
Layer 3: 1 slit green chilli, 1/2 tsp salt, a pinch each (asafoetida, turmeric powder), 1/4 cup finely chopped coconut

Cook on high for 2 whistles or 4 minutes. Release pressure. Mash. Mix in 1 tbsp bottled tadka.

Wednesday: Chettinad Kizhangu Masiyal

Prep.: Take 2 cups tubers peeled and chopped small (wild yam, colocasia, elephant foot yam). Soak in buttermilk/tamarind water overnight. Drain. Mix in 1 tbsp tamarind paste, 1/4 tsp turmeric.

In a 2L Pressure Baker, layer as below:
Layer 1: 2 tbsp oil, 1 tbsp water
Layer 2: 1 cup chopped shallots, 3 chopped garlic cloves, 5 curry leaves
Layer 3: Tubers
Layer 4: 2 chopped green chillies, 1/2 tsp salt

Cook on high for 4 whistles or 5 minutes. Let pressure settle. Mash. Mix in 1 tbsp bottled tadka, 1 tsp lemon juice.

Thursday: Fruit Masiyal

In a 2L Pressure Baker, layer as below:
Layer 1: 2 tbsp oil
Layer 2: 2 cups chopped fruits (tomato, mango, pineapple)
Layer 3: 1/2 cup cooked dal, 1/2 tsp salt, a pinch each (asafoetida, turmeric powder), 1 slit green chilli

Cook on high for 4 whistles or 5 minutes. Release pressure. Mash. Mix in 1/2 cup water, 1tbsp bottled tadka.

Friday: Sprouts Masiyal

In a 2L Pressure Baker, layer as below
Layer 1: 1tbsp ghee, 1/4 cup water
Layer 2: 2 cups sprouts
Layer 3: 1/2tsp salt, a pinch each (asafoetida, turmeric powder), 1 slit green chilli

Cook on high for 4 whistles or 5 minutes. Let pressure settle. Mash. Mix in 1/2 cup water, 1tbsp bottled tadka.

Saturday: Spice/Herb-based Masiyal

In a 2L Pressure Baker, layer as below:
Layer 1: 2tbsp oil
Layer 2: 1/2 cup shallots
Layer 3: 1 cup chopped (garlic/ginger) or 2 cups chopped herbs (mint/cilantro)
Layer 4: 1tsp each (tamarind paste, jaggery), 1/2tsp salt, a pinch of turmeric powder, 1 slit green chilli

Cook on high for 2 whistles or 4 minutes. Release pressure. Mash. Mix in 1/2 cup water, 1tbsp bottled tadka.

Sunday: Mixed Veg Masiyal

In a 2L Pressure Baker, layer as below:
Layer 1: 1/4 cup water, 1tbsp ghee
Layer 2: 2 cups chopped mixed vegetables
Layer 3: 1tsp tamarind paste, 1/2tsp salt, a pinch each (asafoetida, turmeric powder), 2 slit green chillies

Cook on high for 3 whistles or 5 minutes. Release pressure. Mash. Mix in 1/2 cup water, 1tbsp bottled tadka.

Common tadka:

Mustard seeds, urad dal, dry red chillies, curry leaves, thalippu vadagam (sun-dried spiced lentil paste) in oil.

SOUTH INDIAN PODI (DRY CHUTNEYS/SPICED LENTIL POWDER)

Base: Roasted Lentils/Seeds/Nuts
Flavouring: Spices
Additives: Coconut, Jaggery, Tamarind, Garlic

Monday: Instant Podi

Blend 1/2 cup roasted gram, 3 dry red chillies, 1/2tsp each (cumin, salt) to a powder.

Tuesday: Paruppu Podi (Roasted Lentil-based Podi)

See p. 190 for recipe.

Wednesday: Dry Herb-based Podi

Blend 1/4 cup each roasted (gram, dal), 1/2 cup dried herbs (curry leaves, mint), 3 dry red chillies, 1/2tsp each (cumin, salt) to a powder.

Thursday: Spice-based Podi

Roast 1/4 cup each (pepper, cumin), 1tbsp roasted dal, 1/4tsp salt, a pinch of asafoetida. Blend to a powder.

Friday: Thengai Molagapodi (Coconut-based Podi)

See p. 190 for recipe.

Saturday: Ellu/Sesame Podi (Seed-based Podi)

Roast 1/4 cup roasted (dal, sesame seeds), 4 dry red chillies, 1/2tsp salt, a pinch of asafoetida. Blend to a powder.

Sunday: Nut-based Podi

Blend 1/2 cup roasted nuts (peanut, cashew), 1tsp each (coriander, cumin), 3 dry red chillies, 2 garlic cloves, with 1/2tsp each (tamarind, salt) to a powder.

Tips

- Blend to a coarse or fine powder.
- Use as garnish over dry curries.
- Mix into gravies as a thickening agent/dal substitute.
- Mix with oil/ghee to make an instant dip to accompany rice/dosa/idli.
- Mix in with bottled tadka to make a universal slurry garnish.
- Mix in with mashed starchy vegetables to make vegetable podis.
- Lasts months unrefrigerated.
- Can blend in sun-dried vegetables (Turkey berries, nightshade berries), sun-dried flowers (neem), dry spices (ginger, garlic powder).
- Can blend in sun-dried prawns/fish for non-vegetarian versions.

PACHADI (SWEET AND SOUR STEW)

Base: Chillies, Jaggery, Tamarind
Flavouring: Bottled Tadka (p. 26), Spices
Additives: Vegetables, Coconut Paste, Mustard Paste

Monday: Coconut-based Pachadi

Prep.: Blend 1/4 cup chopped coconut, 1tbsp jaggery, 1tsp each (mustard seed, tamarind paste, oil), 1 green chilli, 1/2tsp salt to a paste.

In a 2L Pressure Baker, layer as below:
Layer 1: 1/4 cup water
Layer 2: 2 cups chopped vegetables of your choice

Layer 4: 1/2tsp salt, a pinch of turmeric powder
Layer 5: Coconut paste (see prep.)

Cook on high for 2 whistles or 5 minutes. Release pressure. Mix everything with 1tsp bottled tadka, 1/4 cup water.

Tuesday: Yogurt-based Pachadi

Blend 1/4 cup chopped coconut, 1 green chilli, 1/2tsp salt, 1/4tsp cumin. Mix 1 cup grated salad vegetables (carrot, cucumber, onion), 1 cup yogurt, 1/2tsp sugar, 1tsp bottled tadka.

Wednesday: Jaggery-based Pachadi

In a 2L Pressure Baker, layer as below:
Layer 1: 1/4 cup water
Layer 2: 2 cups chopped vegetables, 2 finely chopped green chillies
Layer 3: 2tbsp jaggery, 1tsp tamarind paste
Layer 4: 1/2tsp salt, a pinch of turmeric powder

Cook on high for 2 whistles or 5 minutes. Release pressure. Mix everything with 1tsp bottled tadka, 1/4 cup water.

Thursday: Nut/Seed-based Pachadi

Blend 1/4 cup roasted sesame/peanut, 1tbsp jaggery, 1tsp tamarind paste, 3 dry red chillies, 1/2tsp salt. Mix in 1 cup chopped salad vegetables, 1tsp bottled tadka.

Friday: Dal-based Pachadi

Blend 4 green chillies, 3tbsp spiced lentil powder, 1tsp tamarind paste, 1/2tsp each (cumin, salt), 2 garlic cloves to a paste. Mix in 2 cups chopped salad vegetables, 1tsp bottled tadka.

Saturday: Spinach-based Pachadi

Prep.: Blend 1/4 cup roasted sesame/peanut, 1tsp tamarind paste, 1tbsp jaggery, 2 green chillies, 1/2tsp salt.

In a 2L Pressure Baker, layer as below:
Layer 1: 1/4 cup water
Layer 2: 4 cups finely chopped spinach
Layer 3: Spice paste (see prep.)

Cook on high for 2 whistles or 4 minutes. Release pressure. Mash and mix in 1tsp bottled tadka, 1/4 cup water.

Sunday: Fruit-based Pachadi

In a 2L Pressure Baker, layer as below:
Layer 1: 1/4 cup water
Layer 2: 2 cups chopped fruits (mango/apple/pineapple)
Layer 3: 2tbsp tamarind paste, 1/2tsp salt, 2 slit green chillies

Cook on high for 2 whistles or 5 minutes. Release pressure. Mash and mix in 1tsp bottled tadka.

Common tadka:

Mustard seeds, dry red chillies, curry leaves, urad dal in oil.

Tips

- Can add other souring agents in place of tamarind.
- Can add other sweeteners in place of sugar.

Drinks/Desserts Module

MUGHAL SHARBAT (FLAVOURED SYRUPS)

Base: Sugar Syrup
Flavouring: Herbs, Spices
Additives: Lemon Juice, Alcohol, Condensed Milk, Cream

Monday: Flower-based Sharbats

Rose/Hibiscus/Jasmine

In a 2L Pressure Baker, add 2 cups each (sugar, water, fresh edible flowers) or 1/4 cup dry edible flowers.

Cook on high for 4 whistles or 8 minutes. Let pressure settle. Strain and bottle.

Tuesday: Herb-based Sharbats

Mint, basil, oregano, lemongrass, pandan leaves, dill, thyme, tarragon, rosemary

In a 2L Pressure Baker, add 2 cups each (sugar, water, fresh herbs) or 2tbsp dry herbs.

Cook on high for 4 whistles or 8 minutes. Let pressure settle. Strain and bottle.

Wednesday: Root/Bark-based Sharbats

Vetiver, nannari, ginger, young turmeric, cinnamon

In a 2L Pressure Baker, add 2 cups each (sugar, water), 1 cup crushed roots.

Cook on high for 4 whistles or 8 minutes. Let pressure settle. Strain and bottle.

Thursday: Spice-based Sharbats

Cardamom, fennel, aniseed, cumin, juniper berries, cloves, sage, coriander seeds, pepper, dry red chillies

In a 2L Pressure Baker, add 2 cups each (sugar, water), 1/4 cup spices.

Cook on high for 4 whistles or 8 minutes. Let pressure settle. Strain and bottle.

Friday: Dry Fruit-based Sharbats

Kokkum, dried plums, raisins, berries, apricot, cherries

In a 2L Pressure Baker, add 2 cups each (sugar, water), 1 cup chopped dry fruits.

Cook on high for 4 whistles or 8 minutes. Let pressure settle. Bottle.

Saturday: Fruit Zest-based Sharbats

Lemon zest, orange zest, citron zest, lime zest

In a 2L Pressure Baker, add 2 cups each (sugar, water), 1/4 cup fruit zest.

Cook on high for 4 whistles or 8 minutes. Let pressure settle. Bottle.

Sunday: Fruit-based Sharbats

Raw mango, gooseberry, pineapple, falsa, peach, sour apples

In a 2L Pressure Baker, add 2 cups each (sugar, water), 1 cup chopped fruits.

Cook on high for 4 whistles or 8 minutes. Let pressure settle. Bottle.

Serving tips:

- Pour over ice cream or fruit salad as a garnish.
- Blend with milk into a milkshake.
- Can mix in soaked basil seeds for texture.
- Can mix in black salt, roasted cumin powder.
- Can mix in chilled/carbonated water, chopped fruits.
- Can replace sugar with jaggery.

Extending sharbats:

- Mix in alcohol with sharbat to make liqueur.
- Mix in instant coffee powder to make infused decoctions/coffee liqueur.
- Mix in heavy cream and whisky to make Irish cream.
- Mix in chocolate sauce and alcohol to make chocolate liqueur.

NORTH INDIAN KHEER (SWEET MILK PUDDING)

Base: Milk/Coconut Milk, Sugar/Jaggery
Flavouring: Cardamom, Cinnamon, Edible Camphor, Saffron
Additives: Fruits, Vegetables, Lentils, Grains, Nuts

Monday: Classic Kheer

In a 2L Pressure Baker, layer as below:
Layer 1: 1/4 cup water, 1tbsp ghee
Layer 2: 1 cup chopped fruits (banana, mango, jackfruit, sapota, apple)
Layer 3: A pinch of cardamom powder

Cook on high for 2 whistles or 5 minutes. Release pressure. Mash coarsely. Mix in 2 cups milk, 2tbsp sugar. If using citrus fruits, wait till it cools and mix in cold milk.

Tuesday: Vegetable Kheer

In a 2L Pressure Baker, layer as below:
Layer 1: 1/4 cup water, 1tbsp ghee
Layer 2: 1 cup chopped vegetables (carrot, potato, zucchini, squash, bottle gourd)
Layer 3: A pinch of cardamom powder

Cook on high for 2 whistles or 5 minutes. Release pressure. Mash coarsely. Mix in 2 cups milk, 2tbsp sugar. Avoid strongly flavoured vegetables like ladyfinger, brinjal, bitter gourd, drumsticks, etc.

Wednesday: Grain-based Kheer

Prep.: Soak 1/4 cup rice (or other grains) for 1 hour.

In a 2L Pressure Baker, add 1tbsp ghee, 1/4 cup each (water, milk), soaked grains, a pinch of cardamom powder, 6 saffron strands.

Cook on high for 3 whistles or 6 minutes. Let pressure settle. Mash coarsely. Mix in 2 cups milk, 2tbsp sugar.

Thursday: Lentil Kheer

Prep.: Soak 1/4 cup chana/moong/masoor/tuvar dal for 2 hours.

In a 2L Pressure Baker, layer as below:
Layer 1: 1/4 cups water, 1tbsp ghee
Layer 2: Dal
Layer 3: A pinch of cardamom powder

Cook on high for 3 whistles or 6 minutes. Let pressure settle. Mash coarsely. Mix in 2 cups milk, 2tbsp sugar. If adding jaggery, do when kheer has cooled.

Friday: Processed Starch Kheer

In a 2L Pressure Baker, layer as below:
Layer 1: 1tbsp ghee
Layer 2: 1/2 cup each (water, milk)
Layer 3: PIP – 1/4 cup (rava/vermicelli/poha/soaked sago/oats), 1 cup water, a pinch of cardamom powder

Cook on high for 3 whistles or 6 minutes. Let pressure settle. Mix everything with 1 cup milk, 2tbsp sugar.

Saturday: Rasayana (No-cook Kheer)

Mash 1 cup fruits. Mix in a pinch of cardamom powder, 2 cups milk, 1tbsp sugar.

Sunday: Nuts/Seed-based Kheer

Prep.: Soak 1/4 cup nuts/seeds (cashew, almond, pistachio, walnut) overnight.

In a 2L Pressure Baker, layer as below:
Layer 1: 1/4 cup water, 1tbsp ghee
Layer 2: Soaked nuts
Layer 3: A pinch of cardamom powder

Cook on high for 3 whistles or 6 minutes. Let pressure settle. Blend everything with 1tbsp ghee, 2 cups milk, 2tbsp sugar.

Tips

- Can mix in condensed milk for a richer taste.
- Can add 1tbsp Dulce de Leche for a caramelized flavour.
- Can add tadka of nuts, dry fruits, coconut slivers, cinnamon, cardamom as garnish.
- Can blend with cream/butter/ghee for emulsification.
- Can replace milk with coconut milk and sugar with jaggery for making pradhaman.

- Can replace sugar with dates/dry fig puree/honey/sweeteners of your choice.
- Can replace milk with plant milk for a vegan version.

SOUTH INDIAN KESARI (SWEETENED GRITS)

Base: Processed Grain
Flavouring: Spices
Additives: Fruits, Milk

Monday: Classic Rava Kesari

In a 2L Pressure Baker, add 2 cups water, 3tbsp ghee, 1/2 cup sugar, 5 saffron strands or a pinch of synthetic colour, 2 crushed cardamom pods.

Cook on high for 1 whistle or 5 minutes. Release pressure. Mix in 1/2 cup double-roasted rava. Close and rest for 15 minutes.

Tuesday: Paal Kesari (Milk-based Kesari)

In a 2L Pressure Baker, add 1 cup water, 1 cup milk, 3tbsp ghee, 1/2 cup sugar, 5 saffron strands or a pinch of synthetic colour, 2 crushed cardamom pods.

Cook on high for 1 whistle or 5 minutes. Let pressure settle. Mix in 1/2 cup double-roasted rava. Close and rest for 15 minutes.

Wednesday: Fruit Kesari

In a 2L Pressure Baker, add 1.5 cup water, 1/2 cup chopped fruits/fruit pulp, 3tbsp ghee, 1/2 cup sugar, 2 crushed cardamom pods.

Cook on high for 1 whistle or 5 minutes. Release pressure. Mix in 1/2 cup double-roasted rava. Close and rest for 15 minutes.

Thursday: Vermicelli Kesari

In a 2L Pressure Baker, add 2 cups water, 3tbsp ghee, 1 cup roasted vermicelli, 1/2 cup sugar, 2 crushed cardamom pods.

Cook on high for 2 whistles or 6 minutes. Let pressure settle. Mix everything.

Friday: Poha Kesari

Prep.: Blend 2 cups poha to a coarse powder.

In a 2L Pressure Baker, add 2 cups water, 3tbsp ghee, 1 cup sugar, 5 saffron strands or a pinch of synthetic colour, 2 crushed cardamom pods.

Cook on high for 1 whistle or 5 minutes. Release pressure. Mix in poha. Close and rest for 15 minutes.

Saturday: Oats Kesari

In a 2L Pressure Baker, add 2 cups water, 3tbsp ghee, 1 cup sugar, 5 saffron strands or a pinch of synthetic colour, 2 crushed cardamom pods.

Cook on high for 1 whistle or 5 minutes. Release pressure. Mix in 2 cups quick cooking-oats. Close and rest for 15 minutes.

Sunday: Fusion Kesari

In a 2L Pressure Baker, add 2 cups water, 3tbsp ghee, 1/2 cup sugar, 5 saffron strands or a pinch of synthetic colour, 2 crushed cardamom pods.

Cook on high for 1 whistle or 5 minutes. Release pressure. Mix in 1/2 cup double-roasted rava, 1/4 cup powder (cashew/almond powder, Horlicks, Milo, Ovaltine). Close and rest for 15 minutes.

Tips

- Can add dry fruits/nuts.
- Can mix in sweet tadka (cinnamon, cardamom, cloves, dry fruits, nuts in ghee).
- Can mix in cocoa powder/grated chocolate for Chocolate Kesari.
- Can mix in coconut milk/plant milk/fruit juices/coconut water after cooking.
- Can use other roasted grain grits as long as they are not too big.

Dal (*p. 144*)

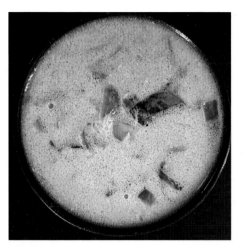

Sri Lankan Hodhi (*p. 123*)

Bengali Dalna (*p. 117*)

South Indian Sambar (*p. 130*)

Telugu Stuffed Brinjal (*p. 37*)

Marathi Zunka (*p. 107*)

Mumbai Pav Bhaji (*p. 101*)

amil Paruppu Usilii (*p. 98*)

Gothsu (*p. 187*)

piced Legumes (*p. 60*)

What's in your fridge: palak (*p. 212*)

Thogayal (*p. 183*)

Kerala Pulisseri (*p. 127*)

Mughlai Pulav (*p. 158*)

Aloo Potol Posto (*p. 147*)

Herb-based Rasam (*p. 56*)

Mexican Burrito Bowl (*p. 167*)

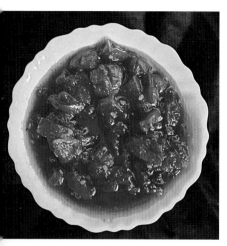

ruit Launji (*p. 150*)

Pachadi (*p. 194*)

alad (*p. 57*)

Mughal Sharbat (*p. 197*)

Tava Pulav (*p. 21*)

Mysore Pak (*p. 43*)

Kadhai Mixed Vegetable (*p. 67*)

Pasta Arrabbiata (*p. 42*)

South Indian One-shot Thali (*p. 236*)

Photo credits: Ranjitha Jeurkar, Visalakshi Venkataraman, Srilakshmi Anand, Shweta Nehra, Tazin Faiz, Ashwini B., Reena Patel

SECTION V
WHAT'S IN YOUR FRIDGE

SECTION V

Recipe by Ingredient

Spice up your week using one base element in seven different ways

POTATO

Base: Potato
Flavouring: Spices, Bottled Tadka (p. 26)
Additives: Curry Pastes, Other Edibles

Monday: Continental Mashed Potato

In a 2L Pressure Baker, layer as below:
Layer 1: 1/4 cup milk, 1tbsp butter
Layer 2: 250g potato chopped small

Cook on high for 4 whistles or 5 minutes. Let pressure settle.
Mash with 1/2tsp each (salt, pepper). Mix in 1tsp chopped cilantro.

Tuesday: Baby Potato Fry with Egg/Paneer

In a 2L Pressure Baker, layer as below:
Layer 1: 3tbsp oil
Layer 2: 250g baby potato pricked all over, 2 well-washed eggs
Layer 3: PIP – 1/2tsp each (chilli, cumin, pepper), 2tsp oil

Cook on high for 4 whistles or 5 minutes. Let pressure settle. Remove
eggs and inner vessel. Drain oil. Peel and chop eggs. Mix everything.
Vegetarians can replace eggs with 150g (soya chunks/paneer) in PIP.

Wednesday: Kaara Kari

In a 2L Pressure Baker, layer as below:
Layer 1: 3tbsp oil
Layer 2: 250g peeled and chopped potato
Layer 3: PIP – 1tsp oil mixed with 1/2tsp each (salt, chilli powder), a pinch of turmeric powder

Cook on high for 4 whistles or 6 minutes. Let pressure settle. Remove PIP. Drain oil. Mix everything.

Thursday: Potato Raita

In a 2L Pressure Baker, layer as below:
Layer 1: 1/4 cup water
Layer 2: 250g chopped potato

Cook on high for 4 whistles or 6 minutes. Let pressure settle. Mix in 1 cup whisked yogurt, 1/2tsp salt, 1/4tsp each (chilli powder, cumin powder).

Friday: Potato Podimas

In a 2L Pressure Baker, layer as below:
Layer 1: 1/4 cup water
Layer 2: 250g peeled and chopped potato
Layer 3: 1/2tsp salt, a pinch each (turmeric powder, asafoetida), 2 chopped green chillies, 1tsp chopped ginger

Cook on high for 4 whistles or 6 minutes. Let pressure settle. Mash coarsely with 1/4 cup grated coconut. Mix in 1tbsp bottled tadka.

Saturday: Bihari Aloo Chokha

In a 2L Pressure Baker, layer as below:
Layer 1: 1/4 cup water
Layer 2: 250g peeled and chopped potato

Cook on high for 4 whistles or 6 minutes. Let pressure settle. Mash with 1tsp mustard oil, 1/2tsp salt. Mix in 1/4 cup chopped onion, 2 chopped green chillies, 1tbsp chopped cilantro.

Sunday: Continental Potato Soup

In a 2L Pressure Baker, layer as below:
Layer 1: 1/4 cup thin milk
Layer 2: 250g peeled and chopped potato

Cook on high for 4 whistles or 6 minutes. Let pressure settle. Add 2 cups milk, 1tbsp butter, 1/2tsp each (salt, pepper). Blend to a thick soup. Serve with roasted papad.

PANEER

Base: Paneer
Flavouring: Spices, Bottled Tadka (p. 26)
Additives: Curry Pastes, Caramelized Onion/Tomato (p. 29), Other Edibles

Monday: Kadhai Paneer

In a 2L Pressure Baker, layer as below:
Layer 1: 3tbsp oil
Layer 2: 1/2 cup each (onion petals, deseeded tomato) cut to stamp-size, 2 slit chillies
Layer 3: 1 cup carrot sliced into coins
Layer 4: 1 cup mixed vegetables (capsicum, mushrooms, cauliflower, broccoli) cut to bite sizes
Layer 5: 1 cup bite-sized paneer mixed with 1/2tsp each (salt, garam masala powder), 1tsp kasuri methi

Cook on high for 2 whistles or 5 minutes. Release pressure. Mix everything.

Tuesday: Lazy Paneer Bhurji

In a 2L Pressure Baker, add 500ml full fat milk, 1/4 cup each (chopped herbs [mint, cilantro], sour yogurt), 1/2tsp each (garam masala, chilli powder, cumin powder, salt). Mix well.
Cook on high for 2 whistles or 6 minutes. Let settle. Strain out whey.
Mix in 1/2 cup each finely chopped (onion, tomato), 1tsp each (kasuri methi, oil), 1 chopped green chilli.

Wednesday: Shahi Paneer Korma

Prep.: Mix 1 cup chopped paneer with 1tsp ginger-garlic paste, 1/4tsp each (salt, chilli powder). Blend 1/4 cup chopped nuts (cashews/almonds/coconut), 1tbsp each (raisins, roasted seeds [poppy/sesame]), 1 green chilli 1/2tsp each (salt, garam masala powder), 1tsp each (herbs [kasuri methi, mint], ghee), 2tbsp water to a thick paste.

In a 2L Pressure Baker, layer as below:
Layer 1: 2tbsp oil/ghee/butter
Layer 2: 1/2 cup each chopped (onion, tomato) arranged in bull's-eye method
Layer 3: PIP – spiced paneer, spice paste

Cook on high for 3 whistles or 4 minutes. Release pressure. Mix everything with 1/2 cup milk.

Thursday: Achari Paneer

Prep.: Mix 1 cup chopped paneer with 3tbsp pickle, 1tsp ginger-garlic paste.

In a 2L Pressure Baker, layer as below:
Layer 1: 2tbsp oil/ghee/butter
Layer 2: 1/2 cup each chopped (onion, tomato) arranged in bull's-eye method
Layer 3: PIP – spiced paneer

Cook on high for 3 whistles or 4 minutes. Release pressure. Mix everything.

Friday: Palak Paneer

Prep.: Mix 1 cup chopped paneer with 1tsp ginger-garlic paste, 1/2tsp each (coriander, cumin powder, salt, garam masala powder).

In a 2L Pressure Baker, layer as below:
Layer 1: 1/4 cup water
Layer 2: 4 cups chopped spinach, 2 chopped green chillies
Layer 3: Spiced paneer

Cook on high for 2 whistles or 4 minutes. Release pressure. Remove paneer. Blend spinach with 1tbsp butter. Mix in paneer.

Saturday: Paneer Salad

Mix 1 cup chopped paneer with 1tsp (lemon juice, pepper), 1/2tsp salt. Add 1/2 cup each chopped (onion, tomato, cucumber), 1/4 cup hung yogurt/salad dressing, 1tbsp each chopped (nuts, dry fruits). Mix everything.

Sunday: Mix Vegetable Paneer Masala

In a 2L Pressure Baker, layer as below:
Layer 1: 1/4 cup water
Layer 2: 1 cup chopped mixed vegetables
Layer 3: 1 cup paneer
Layer 4: 1/4 cup each caramelized (onion, tomato) mixed with 1tsp herbs (kasuri methi, mint), 1/2tsp each (salt, chilli powder, garam masala powder)
Layer 5: 1/4tsp favourite spice powders/spice mix (optional)

Cook on high for 2 whistles or 4 minutes. Release pressure. Mix everything with 1/4 cup cream.

Tips

- Soak paneer in warm water/milk if too hard.
- Can also mix in paneer after cooking, to cook in retained heat.
- Can replace paneer with tofu/soaked soy chunks for a vegan version.
- Mix drained whey water into curries, soups or drink mixed with buttermilk.

PALAK (SPINACH)

Base: Spinach
Flavouring: Spices, Bottled Tadka (p. 26)
Additives: Curry Paste, Other Edibles

Monday: Palak Stir-fry

In a 2L Pressure Baker, layer as below:
Layer 1: 1tbsp oil
Layer 2: 4 cups chopped spinach
Layer 3: 2 chopped green chillies, 1/2tsp salt
Layer 4: 1/4 cup roasted gram flour/grated coconut

Cook on high for 2 whistles or 4 minutes. Release pressure. Mix everything with 1tbsp bottled tadka.

Tuesday: Palak Paneer

In a 2L Pressure Baker, layer as below:
Layer 1: 2tbsp oil
Layer 2: 1/2 cup chopped (onion, deseeded tomato) arranged in bull's eye method, 2 slit chillies
Layer 3: 4 cups finely chopped spinach, 1tsp ginger-garlic paste, 1/2tsp each (salt, garam masala powder)
Layer 4: PIP – 1 cup chopped paneer/tofu

Cook on high for 3 whistles or 5 minutes. Release pressure. Remove paneer. Mash spinach. Mix everything with 1tbsp bottled tadka.

Wednesday: Dal Palak

Prep.: Soak 1/4 cup dal (moong/masoor/chana/tuvar) in water for 2 hours. Drain.

In a 2L Pressure Baker, layer as below:
Layer 1: 1/4 cup water, 1tbsp oil
Layer 2: Dal
Layer 3: 4 cups chopped spinach
Layer 4: 2 chopped green chillies, 1/2tsp salt, a pinch of asafoetida

Cook on high for 3 whistles or 5 minutes. Release pressure. Mix everything with 1tbsp bottled tadka.

Thursday: Palak Subji

In a 2L Pressure Baker, layer as below:
Layer 1: 2tbsp water, 1tbsp oil
Layer 2: 1 cup chopped vegetables/sprouts
Layer 3: 4 cups finely chopped spinach
Layer 4: 2 chopped green chillies, 1/2tsp each (salt, ginger-garlic paste, garam masala powder)

Cook on high for 3 whistles or 5 minutes. Release pressure. Mix everything with 1tbsp bottled tadka.

Friday: Keerai Molagootal

Prep.: Blend 1/4 cup chopped coconut, 1 dry red chilli, 1/2tsp each (salt, cumin), 1tbsp each (roasted urad dal, water), a pinch of turmeric powder to a paste.

In a 2L Pressure Baker, layer as below:
Layer 1: 1/4 cup water

Layer 2: 4 cups chopped spinach (any variety)
Layer 3: Spiced coconut paste, 1/4 cup cooked dal

Cook on high for 2 whistles or 5 minutes. Release pressure. Mash well. Mix in 1/4 cup water, 1tbsp bottled tadka

Saturday: Anda Palak

In a 2L Pressure Baker, layer as below:
Layer 1: 1/4 cup water
Layer 2: 4 cups finely chopped spinach
Layer 3: 1tsp ginger-garlic paste, 1/2tsp each (salt, garam masala powder), 2 green chillies
Layer 4: 3 well-washed eggs

Cook on high for 3 whistles or 5 minutes. Release pressure. Let eggs cool. Peel and chop egg. Mash spinach. Mix everything.

Sunday: Palak Pulav

Prep.: Soak 1 cup basmati rice in water for 30 minutes. Drain. Mix 6 cups chopped spinach, 1tsp each (garam masala powder, chilli powder, salt), 1tbsp ginger-garlic paste, 2 slit green chillies.

In a 2L Pressure Baker, layer as below:
Layer 1: 1tbsp ghee, 1/4 cup water
Layer 2: Half of the spiced spinach (see prep.)
Layer 3: Rice
Layer 4: Cover with remaining spiced spinach

Cook on high for 3 whistles or 7 minutes. Let pressure settle. Mix everything, fluff up and serve.

Common tadka:

Mustard seeds, cumin seeds, dry red chillies in oil.

Tips

- All edible greens can be cooked the same way.
- Finely chop spinach and mash for brighter colour. Blending dulls colour.

CHICKEN

Base: Chicken
Flavouring: Spices, Bottled Tadka (p. 26)
Additives: Curry Pastes, Caramelized Onion/Tomato (p. 29), Other Edibles

Monday: Chicken Masala

Prep.: Marinate 250g chopped chicken with 1tsp ginger-garlic paste, 1/4tsp each (salt, chilli powder, turmeric powder).

In a 2L Pressure Baker, layer as below:
Layer 1: 2tbsp oil/ghee/butter
Layer 2: Spiced chicken
Layer 3: 1/4 cup each caramelized (onion, tomato) mixed with 1tsp herbs (kasuri methi, mint), 1/4tsp each (salt, chilli powder, garam masala powder)
Layer 4: 1/4tsp favourite spice powders/spice mix (optional)

Cook on high for 5 whistles or 6 minutes. Let pressure settle. Mix everything with 1/2 cup water (optional).

Tuesday: Chicken Kuruma

Prep.: Marinate 250g chopped chicken with 1tsp ginger-garlic paste, 1/4tsp each (salt, chilli powder, turmeric powder). Blend 1/4 cup chopped nuts (cashews/almonds/coconut), 1 green chilli, 1tbsp roasted seeds (poppy/sesame), 1tsp each (herbs [kasuri methi, mint], ghee) 1/2tsp each (salt, garam masala powder), 2tbsp water to a thick paste.

In a 2L Pressure Baker, layer as below:
Layer 1: 2tbsp oil/ghee/butter
Layer 2: Spiced chicken
Layer 3: Spice paste (see prep.)
Layer 4: 1/4tsp favourite spice powders/spice mix (optional)
Layer 5: 2tbsp caramelized onion/tomato (optional)

Cook on high for 5 whistles or 6 minutes. Let pressure settle. Mix everything with 1/2 cup milk/coconut milk (optional).

Wednesday: Chicken Achari

Prep.: Marinate 250g chopped chicken with 1tsp ginger-garlic paste, 1/4tsp each (salt, chilli powder, turmeric powder).

In a 2L Pressure Baker, layer as below:
Layer 1: 2tbsp oil/ghee/butter
Layer 2: Spiced chicken
Layer 3: 1/4 cup favourite pickle/thokku
Layer 4: 1/4tsp favourite spice powders/spice mix (optional)
Layer 5: 2tbsp caramelized onion/tomato (optional)

Cook on high for 5 whistles or 6 minutes. Let pressure settle. Mix everything.

Thursday: Chutney Chicken

Prep.: Marinate 250g chopped chicken with 1tsp ginger-garlic paste, 1/4tsp each (salt, chilli powder, turmeric powder).

In a 2L Pressure Baker, layer as below:
Layer 1: 2tsp oil/ghee/butter
Layer 2: Spiced chicken
Layer 3: 1/2 cup favourite chutney/ready-made curry paste
Layer 4: 1/4tsp favourite spice powders/spice mix (optional)
Layer 5: 2tbsp caramelized onion/tomato (optional)

Cook on high for 5 whistles or 6 minutes. Let pressure settle. Mix everything.

Friday: Chicken Saagwala

Prep.: Marinate 250g chopped boneless chicken with 1tsp ginger-garlic paste, 1/4tsp each (salt, chilli powder, turmeric powder).

In a 2L Pressure Baker, layer as below:
Layer 1: 2tbsp oil/ghee/butter
Layer 2: Spiced chicken
Layer 3: 1/4tsp favourite spice powders/spice mix (optional)
Layer 4: 2tbsp caramelized onion/tomato (optional)
Layer 5: PIP – add 4 cups chopped spinach, 1/2tsp each (salt, garam masala powder), 2 green chillies

Cook on high for 5 whistles or 6 minutes. Release pressure. Blend spinach. Mix everything with 1/2 cup water (optional).

Saturday: Chicken Dhansak

Prep.: Marinate 250g boneless chicken chopped small with 1tsp ginger-garlic paste, 1/4tsp each (salt, chilli powder, turmeric powder).

In a 2L Pressure Baker, layer as below:
Layer 1: 2tbsp oil/ghee/butter
Layer 2: Spiced chicken
Layer 3: 1/4tsp favourite spice powders/spice mix (optional)
Layer 4: 2tbsp caramelized onion/tomato (optional)
Layer 5: 1/2 cup cooked dal (moong/tuvar/chana/masoor)
Layer 6: PIP – 1/2 cup each chopped big (carrots, squash), 1/2tsp each (salt, garam masala powder, chilli powder)

Cook on high for 5 whistles or 6 minutes. Release pressure. Mix everything with 1/2 cup water (optional).

Sunday: Chicken Keema Salad

In a 2L Pressure Baker, layer as below:
Layer 1: 2tbsp oil/ghee/butter
Layer 2: 250g chopped boneless chicken

Layer 3: 1 cup potato chopped big
Layer 4: 1/2tsp each (salt, chilli powder, ginger-garlic paste)
Layer 5: 2 well-washed eggs

Cook on high for 5 whistles or 6 minutes. Release pressure. Remove eggs. Let cool, peel and chop. Mix everything with 1 cup lettuce, 1/4 cup each chopped (onion, tomato, cucumber, capsicum), 1/2tsp pepper, 1/4 cup hung yogurt/mayonnaise/salad dressing.

Common tadka:

Bay leaf, star anise, cinnamon, cardamom in oil/ghee.

Tips

- Can dilute all with 1/4 cup cream/milk/coconut milk/yogurt/ stock/water.
- Marinate longer, use bigger pieces and squeeze chicken dry before cooking it, if you want a dry curry.
- If spice paste is not thick, place it in an inner vessel to avoid burning.
- Use same template for vegetables/meats/sprouts/fish/seafood by just varying cooking time.

PRAWNS

Base: Prawns
Flavouring: Spices
Additives: Curry Pastes, Caramelized Onion/Tomato (p. 29), Other Edibles

Monday: Prawn Dopyaza

Prep.: Marinate 250g cleaned prawns with 1tbsp ginger-garlic paste, 1tsp chilli powder, 1/4tsp salt. Mix 3tbsp caramelized onion, 1/2tsp each (garam masala powder, cumin powder) to make a thick paste.

In a 2L Pressure Baker, layer as below:
Layer 1: 2tbsp oil
Layer 2: Spiced prawns
Layer 3: Spice paste (see prep.)

Cook on high for 3 whistles or 5 minutes. Release pressure. Mix everything with 2tbsp whisked yogurt/fresh cream.

Tuesday: Ginger/Garlic Prawns with Vegetables

Prep.: Marinate 250g cleaned prawns with 1tbsp ginger-garlic paste, 1tsp chilli powder, 1/2tsp salt.

In a 2L Pressure Baker, layer as below
Layer 1: 2tbsp oil
Layer 2: Spiced prawns, 1tbsp each chopped (ginger, garlic)
Layer 3: 1 cup chopped mixed vegetables
Layer 4: 1tsp each (coriander powder, garam masala powder)

Cook on high for 3 whistles or 5 minutes. Release pressure. Mix everything.

Wednesday: Pesto Prawns

Prep.: Blend 1/2 cup fresh herbs, 1/4 cup nuts (pine nuts/walnut/cashew/almond/peanuts), 2 garlic cloves, 1tbsp oil, 2 green chillies, 1/4tsp salt to a paste. Marinate 250g cleaned prawns with 1tbsp ginger-garlic paste, 1tsp chilli powder, 1/4tsp salt.

In a 2L Pressure Baker, layer as below:
Layer 1: 2tbsp oil
Layer 2: Spiced prawns
Layer 3: Spice paste (see prep.)

Cook on high for 3 whistles or 5 minutes. Release pressure. Mix everything.

Thursday: Chilli Prawns

Marinate 250g cleaned prawns with 1tbsp ginger-garlic paste, 1tsp each (soy sauce, chilli sauce, vinegar).

In a 2L Pressure Baker, layer as below:
Layer 1: 2tbsp oil
Layer 2: 1 cup bite-sized onion petals
Layer 3: Spiced prawns, 6 slit green chillies
Layer 4: PIP – 1 cup bite-sized mixed colour bell peppers

Cook on high for 3 whistles or 5 minutes. Release pressure. Mix everything with 1tbsp dark soy sauce.

Friday: Prawn Korma

Prep.: Marinate 250g cleaned prawns with 1tbsp ginger-garlic paste, 1tsp each (chilli powder, turmeric powder, salt).

In a 2L Pressure Baker, layer as below:
Layer 1: 2tbsp oil
Layer 2: Spiced prawns
Layer 3: 2tbsp each caramelized (onion, tomato)
Layer 4: 3tbsp cashew/almond powder, 1tsp each (cumin powder, garam masala powder)

Cook on high for 3 whistles or 5 minutes. Release pressure. Mix everything with 1/4 cup cream.

Saturday: Prawn Posto (Prawns in Poppy Seed Paste)

Prep.: Soak 2tbsp poppy seeds in water for 2 hours. Drain. Blend caramelized onion, tomato, 2 green chillies, 1/4tsp each (salt, turmeric powder), 1tsp oil into a thick paste. Marinate 250g cleaned prawns with 1tbsp ginger-garlic paste, 1tsp chilli powder, 1/4tsp each (salt, turmeric powder).

In a 2L Pressure Baker, layer as below:
Layer 1: 2tbsp oil
Layer 2: Spiced prawns
Layer 3: 2tbsp each caramelized (onion, tomato)
Layer 4: Posto paste (see prep.)

Cook on high for 3 whistles or 5 minutes. Release pressure. Mix everything.

Sunday: Prawn Pickle

Prep.: Marinate 250g cleaned prawns with 1/2tsp salt, 1/4tsp turmeric powder. Squeeze to remove moisture.

In a 2L Pressure Baker, layer as below:
Layer 1: 1/4 cup oil
Layer 2: 250g prawns
Layer 3: 1tbsp Kashmiri red chilli powder, 1tsp each (cumin powder, coriander powder, mustard powder), 1/2tsp each (fennel powder, garam masala powder)

Cook on high for 3 whistles or 5 minutes. Release pressure. Mix in 1/4 cup vinegar, 1tsp sugar.

Tips

- Can place spice paste in PIP if it is not thick.
- Pat dry/sun dry/fridge dry prawns as much as possible.
- Can add chopped coriander, bottled tadka, julienned ginger, fresh cream as garnish.

EGGS

Base: Spinach
Flavouring: Spices, Bottled Tadka (p. 26)
Additives: Curry Paste, Other Edibles

Monday: Egg Chaat/Egg Salad

In a 2L Pressure Baker, add 1/2 cup water, 6 well-washed eggs.

Cook on high for 2 whistles or 4 minutes. Let pressure settle. Let eggs cool. Peel and chop. Mix in 1/2 cup each chopped (onion, tomato), 3 chopped green chillies, 1/4 cup chopped cilantro, 1/2tsp each (chaat masala, salt, pepper powder). Or mix in salad dressing to convert it into an egg salad.

Tuesday: Egg Drop Soup

In a 2L Pressure Baker, add 3 cups water, 1 cup crushed noodles, tastemaker (optional), 1/2 cup each chopped (carrot, beans), 1/2tsp each (salt, pepper powder).

Cook on high for 1 whistle or 5 minutes. Release pressure. Pour in one beaten egg in a thin stream.

Wednesday: Devilled Eggs

In a 2L Pressure Baker, add 1/2 cup water, 6 well-washed eggs.

Cook on high for 2 whistles or 4 minutes. Let pressure settle. Let eggs cool. Peel and halve. Remove yolks. Mix yolks with 2tsp each (mayonnaise, vinegar, mustard), 1/2tsp each (salt, pepper powder). Spoon yolks into the egg whites.

Thursday: Egg Korma

Prep.: Cut 1/2 cup each chopped (carrot, beans, potato, paneer). Blend 1/4 cup soaked almonds, 1tsp each (ginger-garlic paste, salt), 1/2tsp garam masala powder, 1 green chilli, 2tbsp water to a thick paste.

In a 2L Pressure Baker, layer as below:
Layer 1: 1/4 cup water
Layer 2: Vegetables, 1/2 cup green peas

Layer 3: Nut paste, 5 crushed mint leaves
Layer 4: PIP – 2 eggs

Cook on high for 3 whistles or 5 minutes. Release pressure. Mix everything with 1/2 cup milk/coconut milk.

Friday: Egg Bhurji

In a 2L Pressure Baker, layer as below:
Layer 1: 2tbsp oil
Layer 2: 1 cup chopped onion, 4 chopped green chillies
Layer 3: 1/2tsp each (salt, pepper)

Cook on high for 4 whistles or 4 minutes. Release pressure. Mix everything. Add 2 beaten eggs. Mix and keep closed for 5 minutes.

Saturday: Egg Masala

In a 2L Pressure Baker, layer as below:
Layer 1: 2tbsp oil
Layer 2: 1 cup each chopped (onion, tomato) arranged in bull's-eye method
Layer 3: 1tsp ginger-garlic paste, 1/2tsp each (salt, chilli powder, garam masala powder)
Layer 4: 4 well-washed eggs

Cook on high for 4 whistles or 5 minutes. Let pressure settle. Let eggs cool. Peel and halve. Mash gravy. Pour over eggs.

Sunday: Mutta Aviyal

See p. 71 for recipe.

COOKING WITH NOTHING

Stretching Curries with Spice Paste

Base: Vegetables
Flavouring: Spices
Additives: Curry Paste, Other Edibles

Monday: Tamil Tomato Rasam

In a 2L Pressure Baker, layer as below:
Layer 1: 1/4 cup water
Layer 2: 1/2 cup chopped tomato
Layer 3: PIP – 2tbsp each (coriander powder, cumin powder, pepper, salt), 1tsp turmeric powder, 1 cup water

Cook on high for 4 whistles or 5 minutes. Release pressure. Mix everything with 5 cups water.

Tuesday: Bengali Jhol

In a 2L Pressure Baker, layer as below:
Layer 1: 1/4 cup water
Layer 2: 1/2 cup chopped tomato
Layer 3: PIP – 2tbsp each (panch phoran powder, coriander powder, cumin powder, salt), 3tbsp Kashmiri chilli powder, 1tsp sugar, 1 cup water

Cook on high for 4 whistles or 5 minutes. Release pressure. Mix everything with 5 cups water.

Wednesday: Anglo-Indian Mulligatawny

In a 2L Pressure Baker, layer as below:
Layer 1: 1/4 cup water
Layer 2: 1/2 cup chopped tomato
Layer 3: PIP – 3tbsp pepper, 2tbsp each (coriander powder, cumin powder, salt), 1 cup water

Cook on high for 4 whistles or 5 minutes. Release pressure. Mix everything with 6 cups water/stock.

Thursday: Kongu Pacha Rasam

Blend 1 tomato, 2tbsp each (coriander powder, cumin powder, pepper, salt), 1/2tsp asafoetida, 4 cups water. Mix in 2 cups hot water/water.

Friday: Marathi Tarri

In a 2L Pressure Baker, layer as below:
Layer 1: 1/4 cup water
Layer 2: 1/2 cup chopped tomato
Layer 3: PIP – 2tbsp each (kala masala, coriander powder, cumin powder, salt), 3tbsp Kashmiri chilli powder, 1 cup water

Cook on high for 4 whistles or 5 minutes. Release pressure. Mix everything with 5 cups water.

Saturday: Assamese Jhola

In a 2L Pressure Baker, layer as below:
Layer 1: 1/4 cup water
Layer 2: 1/2 cup chopped tomato
Layer 3: PIP – 2tbsp each (garam masala powder, coriander powder, cumin powder, salt), 3tbsp Kashmiri chilli powder, 1tsp turmeric powder, 1 cup water

Cook on high for 4 whistles or 5 minutes. Release pressure. Mix everything with 5 cups water.

Sunday: Gujarati Osaman

In a 2L Pressure Baker, layer as below:
Layer 1: 1/4 cup water
Layer 2: 1/2 cup chopped tomato

Layer 3: PIP – 2tbsp each (garam masala powder, coriander powder, cumin powder, salt, pepper, Kashmiri chilli powder, jaggery), 1tsp each (turmeric powder, asafoetida), 1 cup water

Cook on high for 4 whistles or 5 minutes. Release pressure. Mix everything with 5 cups water.

BONUS RECIPES

You don't need any vegetable at all, not even the single tomato. The spices alone are good enough!

Milagu Jeera Rasam

In a 2L Pressure Baker, add 2 cups water. PIP – 2tbsp each (coriander powder, salt), 3tbsp each (cumin powder, pepper), 1/2 cup water. Cook on high for 5 whistles or 6 minutes. Release pressure. Mix everything with 3 cups water.

No-name Thin Curry

Choose any masala mix (chana masala/chicken masala/mutton masala, pav bhaji masala). In a 2L Pressure Baker, add 2 cups water. PIP – 2tbsp each (masala mix, coriander powder, salt), 3tbsp each (cumin powder, pepper), 1/2 cup water. Cook on high for 5 whistles or 6 minutes. Release pressure. Mix everything with 3 cups water.

SECTION VI
ONE-SHOT THALIS

From Making a Meal to Cooking a Feast!

From breakfast to dinner, Indian meals have always comprised multiple dishes served together as a thali. With lifestyles getting busier, the number of dishes has slowly decreased to one or two. Even this was sometimes skipped, with rice/ roti/ idli/ dosa being paired with just pickles.

There was a great need to cook multiple dishes together. The concept is not new; earlier, pressure cookers came with vessels that can be stacked over each other. There were two problems with this technique:

- The vegetables invariably became a mush, losing colour, texture, nutrients and flavour.
- A finishing step was required for the dal/ vegetables to be converted into curries.

Among the dilemmas we faced were, how do we keep the dishes separate? Won't everything taste the same? Won't all flavours mix together? Getting the answers to these questions took repeated trials and validations.

Introducing physically separate zones ensured there was no intermingling of flavours. We also learnt to choose combinations carefully, to get the exact flavour profile we wanted. Soon, we found cooking a feast was no different than cooking a single dish once you have ingredients and curry bases ready.

Multiple OPOS techniques had to come together to make this happen:

- Waterless Cooking ensured multiple dishes stayed in their separate zones and did not get mixed up.
- Cut size variation ensured that any combination of vegetables can be cooked together, without overcooking or undercooking.
- Pressure Baking ensured the inherent taste of the ingredients was maximized without reliance on elaborate spice mixes. This is the reason why each dish smells and tastes different, even when cooked together.
- Layering, PIP, Nesting and MPOS (Multiple Pots One Shot) were used to balance cooking times and add curry bases.

When we got comfortable with the concept, the separators were designed. This tool supercharged the technique. OPOS members started innovating by cooking up elaborate thalis.

To cook these thalis, which can feed 2-3 adults, the ingredients are layered in different zones over a water or oil buffer. Other spices and building blocks are layered over them. The building blocks can be OPOS staples or curry bases (tamarind paste, cooked dal, coconut paste, caramelized onion-tomato paste or nut paste). These are Pressure Baked together, removed separately and diluted.

Almost all regional and ethnic Thalis were now rewritten to use this technique offering a ready-to-serve thali in minutes, when you open the pot!

Getting it right

- Balance cooking time by choosing the right vegetables.
- Avoid pairing watery vegetables with starchy ones in different zones, since they need different types of buffer.
- Avoid vegetables like ladyfinger/brinjal/cauliflower/spinach, along with legumes or meat in one-shot thalis.
- Avoid cooking vegetables along with tough meats like mutton/pork.
- To avoid overcooking, use seafood in PIP when pairing with other meats.

- Use smaller chunks of meat. Marinate longer/preferably overnight to tenderize the meat. This also enhances the flavour.
- Pat dry the meat/seafood to avoid water leakage or refrigerate it uncovered overnight to minimize water leakage.
- Do not overfill the pot. It is not advisable to fill the pot with more than 4 cups vegetables (including the spice pastes). This can lead to extended cooking time of over 5 minutes, which overcooks vegetables.
- Adjust buffer according to the dishes chosen. If the actual recipe calls for onion, tomato in the buffer layer, while the other two dishes need water as buffer, it would be better to use caramelized bases instead of layering onion and tomato along with water. Use appropriate cut-size variations of vegetables to balance their cooking time.

5-MINUTE LOW-CARB RAINBOW THALI

In a 2L Pressure Baker, layer as below:
Layer 1: 2tbsp water, 2tsp oil
Place the separators, dividing the base into three zones.

Zone 1
Layer 2: 1 cup chopped beans
Layer 3: 1/4tsp salt, 1tsp tadka

Zone 2
Layer 2: 1 cup chopped carrot
Layer 3: 1/4tsp salt, 1tsp tadka

Zone 3
Layer 2: 1 cup chopped green tomato
Layer 3: 1/4tsp salt, 1tsp tadka
Layer 4: In a plate (place it above the separators) 1 cup mixed sprouts, 1/4tsp salt, 1tsp tadka

Close and cook on high for 3 whistles or 5 minutes. Release pressure. Separate the dishes and serve.

For,

Raita/Dip: Grate 1tbsp each (cucumber, carrot) and mix in 1/2 cup yogurt and a pinch each (salt, cumin powder).

Salad: Slice 1/4 cup each (carrot, radish, cucumber, tomato) to thin discs and mix in a pinch of salt, 1/4tsp lemon juice and 1/2tsp tadka. Serve with buttermilk, nuts and fruits.

Replace/Supplement:

- Sprouts with paneer/chopped spinach.
- Beans, carrot with favourite vegetables.
- Green tomato with favourite semi-ripe fruits.

PAN-INDIAN ONE-SHOT THALI #1

Prep.: Blend 2tbsp coconut, 2tsp mustard, 1tsp poppy seeds, 2 green chillies, 1/2tsp each (salt, sugar), a pinch of turmeric powder.

In a 2L Pressure Baker, layer as below:
Layer 1: 2tbsp oil
Place the separators, dividing the base into three zones.

Zone 1: Keerai Masiyal
Layer 2: 1/4 cup chopped tomato, 1 green chilli
Layer 3: 2 cups chopped spinach
Layer 4: 1/2tsp salt

Zone 2: Olan
Layer 2: 1 torn red chilli, 5 curry leaves, 1/2tsp cumin
Layer 3: 1/2 cup cubed squash
Layer 4: 1/4 cup sprouts

Zone 3: Paneer Phulkopir Shorshe
Layer 2: 1 cup cauliflower
Layer 3: Spice paste

Cook on high for 2 whistles or 5 minutes. Release pressure. Separate dishes.

Zone 1: Keerai Masiyal
Mash and mix in 1 tsp tadka
Zone 2: Olan
Mix in 1/2 cup coconut milk, 1 tsp coconut oil
Zone 3: Bengali Shorshe
Mix 1/2 cup paneer, 1/2 tsp panch phoran tadka, 1/4 cup yogurt

PAN-INDIAN ONE-SHOT THALI #2

Prep.: Blend 2 tbsp each (coconut, cashew), 2 green chillies, 1/2 tsp each (ginger-garlic paste, garam masala powder, salt) to a thick kuruma paste.

In a 2L Pressure Baker, layer as below:
Layer 1: 1/4 cup water
Place the separators, dividing the base into three zones.

Zone 1
Layer 2: 1 cup chopped carrot
Layer 3: PIP – 1/2 cup North Indian Curry Base/Mother Sauce

Zone 2
Layer 2: 1 cup chopped beans
Layer 3: PIP – kuruma paste

Zone 3
Layer 2: 1 cup chopped potato

Cook on high for 3 whistles or 5 minutes. Release pressure. Remove PIP and separators.

You can make:
Dry Curry: Mix 1/2 cup mixed vegetables with 1tsp tadka
Shahi Veg Masala: Mix 1/4 cup each (vegetables, mother sauce), 2tbsp cream
Mixed Veg Masala: Mix 1/4 cup each (vegetables, mother sauce, milk)
Shahi Kuruma: Mix 1/4 cup each (vegetables, nut paste, coconut milk)
Sour Kuruma: Mix 1/4 cup each (vegetables, nut paste, yogurt)
Mixed Veg Curry: Mix remaining vegetables, 2tbsp (nut paste, mother sauce), 1tbsp each (coconut milk, water)

TELUGU ONE-SHOT THALI

In a 2L Pressure Baker, layer as below:
Layer 1: 2tbsp oil
Place the separators, dividing the base into three zones.

Zone 1
Layer 2: 1/4tsp each (mustard, cumin), 1 dry red chilli, 2 curry leaves
Layer 3: 1 cup deseeded and chopped snake gourd
Layer 4: 2 ripe red chillies, 1/4tsp salt, a pinch of asafoetida

Zone 2
Layer 2: 1/4tsp each (mustard, cumin), 1 dry red chilli, 2 curry leaves
Layer 3: 1 cup chopped cabbage, 1 slit green chilli
Layer 4: 1/4tsp salt, a pinch of asafoetida, PIP: 2tbsp each (corn, peas)

Zone 3
Layer 2: 1/4tsp each (mustard, cumin), 1 dry red chilli, 2 curry leaves
Layer 3: 1 cup chopped mixed vegetables
Layer 4: 1tsp salt, 1/4tsp turmeric powder, a pinch of asafoetida
Layer 5: PIP – 1tsp paruppu podi, 1/2tsp each (thengai molagapodi, sambar powder), 4g raw tamarind, 1/4 cup water

Cook on high for 2 whistles or 5 minutes. Release pressure. Remove PIP and separate the dishes.

Zone 1
Perugu Pachadi: Mix 1/2 cup snake gourd, 1/4 cup yogurt.
Podi Kura: Mix remaining snake gourd with 1tbsp thengai molagapodi.
Zone 2
Cabbage Podi Kura: Mix everything with 1/4 cup grated coconut.
Zone 3:
Instant Sambar: Mix PIP contents with 1/2 cup water.
Serve with rice/roti and papad.

NON-VEG ONE-SHOT THALI

In a 2L Pressure Baker, layer as below:
Layer 1: 3tbsp oil
Place the separators, dividing the base into three zones.

Zone 1: Chicken Masala
Layer 2: 1/4 cup chopped onion
Layer 3: 1/2 cup chicken marinated with 1tsp ginger-garlic paste, 1/4tsp turmeric powder, 1/2tsp each (salt, red chilli powder, cumin powder, coriander powder, garam masala powder)

Zone 2: Shahi Chicken
Layer 2: 1/2 inch cinnamon, 2 cardamoms, 2 cloves, 2 slit green chillies (optional)
Layer 3: 1/2 cup chopped chicken marinated with 1tsp ginger-garlic paste, 1/4tsp turmeric powder, 1/2tsp each (salt, pepper)

Zone 3: Palak Chicken
Layer 2: 1/4 cup chopped onions
Layer 3: 1/2 cup chicken marinated with 1tsp ginger-garlic paste, 1/4tsp turmeric powder, 1/2tsp each (salt, red chilli powder, cumin powder, coriander powder, garam masala powder)

In a plate add 1/2 cup chopped spinach/baby spinach

Cook on high for 5 whistles or 5 minutes. Release pressure. Remove PIP and separate the dishes.

Zone 1: Chicken Masala
Mix everything.
Zone 2: Shahi Chicken
Mix in 1/4 cup cream.
Zone 3: Palak Chicken
Blend spinach (optional) and mix all.

ONE-SHOT LOW-CARB THALI

In a 2L Pressure Baker, layer as below:
Layer 1: 2tbsp oil, 4 to 5 torn curry leaves
Place the separators, dividing the base into three zones.

Layer 2
Zone 1: 1 cup chopped radish, a pinch each (salt, turmeric powder), 1/2tsp chilli powder
Zone 2: 1 cup chopped cabbage, a pinch each (salt, turmeric powder)
Zone 3: 2 cups chopped spinach, a pinch of salt

Cook on high for 2 whistles or 4 minutes. Release pressure. Separate the dishes. Meanwhile, blend 1/4 cup chopped coconut, 1 green chilli, 3 garlic cloves, 1/2tsp cumin, 4 curry leaves into a thick CCC paste.

Zone 1: Mix in radishes to make a **Spicy Stir-fry**.
Zone 2: Mix in 1/4 cup CCC paste with cabbage for **Thoran**.
Zone 3: Mix in spinach with 2tbsp each (CCC paste, water), 1/4 cup yogurt and get **Spinach Raita**.

SOUTH INDIAN ONE-SHOT THALI

In a 2L Pressure Baker, layer as below:
Layer 1: 2tbsp oil, 1/2tsp mustard seeds, 4 to 5 torn curry leaves
Place the separators, dividing the base into three zones.

Layer 2
Zone 1: 1 cup finely chopped brinjal, 1 green chilli, 1/8tsp asafoetida, 1/4tsp salt, 1tsp raw tamarind
Zone 2: 1 cup chopped raw banana, 1/4tsp salt, a pinch of turmeric powder
Zone 3: 1 cup chopped carrot, a pinch of salt

Cook on high for 2 whistles or 4 minutes. Release pressure. Separate the dishes. Meanwhile, blend 1/4 cup chopped coconut, 1 green chilli, a pinch of pepper, 1/2tsp cumin into a thick CCC paste

Zone 1: Remove one part of brinjal with the tamarind piece. Mash well, add 2tsp paruppu podi, 1tbsp water for **Gothsu**.
To the other part of brinjal, mix in 1/4 cup curd and make **Mosaru bajji**.
Zone 2: To the raw bananas, add 1tbsp thengai molagapodi, 3tbsp CCC paste, 1/4 cup water to get **Erissery**.
Zone 3: To the carrot, mix in 1tbsp CCC paste and you have **Thoran**.

Plate with rice, ghee, pickle, dessert/fruit.

GRAND THALI (ONA SADHYA)

Fourteen dishes in three rounds of Pressure Baking

Sambar, Mezhukkupuratti, Thoran, Rasam, Erissery, Madhura Kari, Olan, Kurukku Kaalan, Beetroot Pachadi, Pulisseri, Moru Kachiyathu, Kootu Kari, Pradhaman, Aviyal

Prep.:
1. CCC paste: Blend 1 cup chopped/grated coconut with 1tsp each (cumin, oil), 4 green chillies into a thick coarse paste.
2. Varuthu aracha sambar paste: Roast 2 dry red chillies, 1/2tbsp each (coriander, chana dal, coconut), a pinch each (fenugreek powder, cumin powder, asafoetida). Blend with 1tbsp water, 1/2tsp salt. Alternatively, use 3tbsp thengai molagapodi (spiced

roasted coconut). Mix with 1/2 cup cooked dal, 1/2tsp tamarind paste to form a thick patty.

3. Soak 1tbsp black-eyed beans for 1 hour. Drain.

4. Spiced buttermilk: In a small cup, add 1/2 cup thin buttermilk, a pinch each (turmeric powder, cumin powder, fenugreek powder, salt), 2 curry leaves.

Load 1
In a 2L Pressure Baker, layer as below:
Layer 1: 3tbsp water, 1tsp coconut oil
Place the separators, dividing the base into four zones.

Zone 1:
Layer 2: 1/2 cup chopped beans cut into 1.5 inch long pieces

Zone 2:
Layer 2: 1/2 cup chopped carrot cut into thick fingers
Layer 3: Sambar patty (see prep.)

Zone 3:
Layer 2: 1/2 cup chopped cabbage, 1 slit green chilli

Zone 4: 1/4 cup chopped drumstick, 1 whole scooped tomato with rasam mix, 1/4tsp each (salt, pepper, cumin, coriander leaves, tamarind paste, crushed ginger, spiced lentil powder)
Keep a plate on top of separators with the CCC paste (see prep.).

Cook on high for 2 whistles or 5 minutes. Release pressure. Separate vegetables.

Load 2
In a 2L Pressure Baker, layer as below:
Layer 1: 1/4 cup water, 2tsp coconut oil
Place the separators, dividing the base into four zones.

Zone 1
Layer 2: 1 cup chopped yam
Zone 2
Layer 2: 1 cup chopped raw banana
Zone 3
Layer 2: 1/2 cup sprouts
Layer 3: 1 cup chopped squash
Zone 4
Layer 2: Black-eyed beans (see prep.)
Layer 3: 1/2 cup chopped white pumpkin

Cook on high for 2 whistles or 6 minutes. Release pressure. Separate vegetables. See below.

Load 3:
In a 2L Pressure Baker, layer as below:
Layer 1: 2tbsp water
Place the separators, dividing the base into three zones.
Layer 2:
Zone 1: PIP – spiced buttermilk (see prep.)
Zone 2:
Layer 2: 1 cup chopped pineapple
Zone 3:
Layer 2: 1 cup chopped ripe mango
Keep a plate on top of separators with 1/2 cup grated beetroot.

Cook on high for 2 whistles or 5 minutes. Release pressure. Separate vegetables.

Mix and match cooked vegetables to make 14 curries

- **Sambar**: Mix 2tbsp each (carrot, drumstick), cooked dal, spice paste, 1/4 cup water.
- **Mezhukkupuratti**: Mix 1/4 cup beans, 1/2tsp coconut oil, a pinch of salt.

- **Thoran**: Mix 1/2 cup cabbage, 1tbsp CCC paste, a pinch of salt.
- **Rasam**: Mash the tomato filled with spices and mix in 1/4 cup water.
- **Erissery**: Mix 2tbsp each (squash, raw banana, yam) with 1/4tsp salt, 2tbsp thengai molagapodi.
- **Madhura Kari**: Mix 1/4 cup squash, 2tbsp each (CCC paste, yogurt), a pinch of salt.
- **Olan**: Mix 1/4 cup white pumpkin, black-eyed beans, 1/8 cup coconut milk, 1/4tsp each (pepper powder, coconut oil, salt).
- **Kurukku Kaalan**: Mix 1/4 cup each (strained yogurt, raw banana), 2tbsp CCC paste, a pinch each (salt, pepper powder).
- **Beetroot Pachadi**: Mix grated beetroot, 1tbsp CCC paste, a pinch of salt, 2tbsp yogurt.
- **Pulisseri**: Mix pineapples, 2tbsp each (CCC paste, yogurt), a pinch of salt.
- **Moru Kachiyathu**: Remove PIP. Mix and serve as it is.
- **Kootu Kari**: Mix 1/4 cup each (sprouts, yam), 2tbsp CCC paste, 1/4tsp each (pepper, jaggery), a pinch of salt.
- **Pradhaman**: Mix ripe mangoes, 1/4 cup each (coconut milk, condensed milk, powdered jaggery), a pinch of cardamom powder.
- **Aviyal**: Mix remaining vegetables, 2tbsp each (CCC paste, yogurt), 1/4tsp salt, 1tsp oil, 2 curry leaves.

Prepare the following no-cook dishes

- **Parippu**: Mix 1/4 cup pre-prepared dal with 1/4tsp ghee, a pinch of salt.
- **Vellarikka Kichadi**: Mix 1/4 cup each (grated cucumber, yogurt), 1tbsp CCC paste, a pinch of salt.
- **Inji Thayiru**: Mix 1/2 cup yogurt, 2tsp grated ginger, 1tsp chopped chilli, 1/4tsp salt.

- **Maanga Kari**: Mix in 2tbsp chopped raw mango, a pinch of chilli powder and oil.

- **Paruppu Payasam**: Mix 1/4 cup cooked moong dal, 2tbsp powdered jaggery, 1tbsp each (coconut milk, condensed milk), a pinch of cardamom powder.

Arranging the thali

Serve the curries on a banana leaf with choru (rice), ghee, puli inji (pickle), pappadam, banana chips, jackfruit chips, banana, yogurt, salt, sambaaram (buttermilk), semiya payasam.

OPOS Techniques: A Quick Guide

- A is for Attalysis, for strain-free kneading.
- B is for Bottled tadka, for healthy, gunk-free cooking.
- C is for Controlled caramelization, for hands-free sautéing.
- C is for Cold-pressure frying, for healthy frying.
- C is for Controlled evaporation, to deskill ghee-making.
- D is for Dum, to maximize flavour.
- E is for Emulsification for creamy curries.
- G is for Greater surface area, to balance cooking times and stretch out dal.
- H is for Hydro-distillation, to extract maximum flavour from food.
- I is for Inner vessel cooking, to create multiple heating zones.
- J is for Just enough liquid, to reduce water, fuel and food wastage.
- K is for Key building blocks, to create infinite recipes.
- L is for Layering, to create complex recipes in one step.
- M is for Meal planning, to reduce decision fatigue.
- N is for No cutting, to minimize preparation.
- O is for Oil-free cooking.
- P is for Pressure Baking, to make food come alive.
- Q is for Queued cooking, to cook anything with anything.
- R is for Retained heat cooking, to prevent clumping.
- S is for Sugar syrup hack, to deskill sugar syrup consistency.

- U is for Use of cooked bases and finishing spices, to eliminate the raw smell.
- V is for Very long marination, to store cut vegetables.
- X is for Xtended storage, or off-the-grid storage.
- Y is for Yolk colour retention, to eliminate the green ring.
- Z is for Zoned Pressure Baking, to cook a thali at one shot.

Acknowledgements

THANK YOU!

To the OPOS book team – Ashwini B., Visalakshi Venkataraman, Tazin Faiz and Srilakshmi Anand, who made the book happen. They shot the eye-popping pictures (no filters are ever used in OPOS pictures). They made the videos. They collated my rough drafts, edited them and gave the manuscript its current shape. The team is a dream to work with!

To all those who contributed photos and videos – Vidya Kalai, Shweta Nehra, Reena Patel, Dheepika Balasubramanian, Prabha Sridharan, Divya K. Swamy, Roopa Raghav, Radhika Thiagarajan, Sutapa Mukherjee, Ranjitha Jeurkar and Anu Sash.

To the members of OPOS groups, who validated the templates.

To HarperCollins for teaming up with us to publish our first OPOS paperback!

To all of you, heartfelt thanks!

ॐ सर्वे भवन्तु सुखिनः
सर्वे सन्तु निरामयाः

Om Sarve Bhavantu Sukhinah
Sarve Santu Niraamayaah |
Om, May All be Happy, May All be Free from Illness.

About the Author

B. Ramakrishnan passionately believes anyone, anywhere, anytime should be able to cook great food, with great ease. He sold his software company to focus full-time on his passion for cooking. The one-page cookbooks came first. OPOS followed a decade later. He is now a consultant, columnist and CEO of Pizza Republic and OPOS Kitchen. He holds the record for cooking, solo, a ten-course marriage feast for 500 people in 3 hours, using OPOS techniques. His first OPOS e-cookbook, *5-minute Magic*, became an international bestseller.

Learn more about OPOS:
YouTube: https://rb.gy/jlbflz
Facebook: https://rb.gy/j8jt5x
Buy the OPOS Kit https://oposkit.com/
OPOSChef App available for Android and iOS